POVERTY, U. S. A.

THE HISTORICAL RECORD

ADVISORY EDITOR: David J. Rothman

Professor of History, Columbia University

PUBLIC RELIEF
AND PRIVATE CHARITY

JOSEPHINE SHAW LOWELL

Arno Press & The New York Times

NEW YORK   1971

Reprint Edition 1971 by Arno Press Inc.

Reprinted from a copy in
The University of Illinois Library

LC# 76—137176
ISBN 0—405—03115—7

POVERTY, U.S.A.: THE HISTORICAL RECORD
ISBN for complete set: 0-405-03090-8

Manufactured in the United States of America

QUESTIONS OF THE DAY.—No. XIII.

PUBLIC RELIEF

AND

PRIVATE CHARITY

BY

JOSEPHINE SHAW LOWELL

NEW YORK & LONDON
G. P. PUTNAM'S SONS
The Knickerbocker Press
1884

PREFACE.

I have compiled this little book because I believe some such restatement of the principles upon which the Modern methods of Charity are based is needed.

There is not, perhaps, an original thought or suggestion in it :—an important part of it is direct and verbal quotation ; and to every student of the subject it will be apparent that almost the whole of it is taken from the writings of wise men and women who have lived during the past hundred years. Yet I do not apologize for offering it to my fellow workers and the public, for there is nowhere a small book in which the principles underlying our science can be found clearly stated.

I speak of " our science," because fortunately the task of dealing with the poor and degraded has become a science, and has its well defined principles, recognized and conformed to, more or less closely, by all who really give time and thought to the subject.

From all parts of the world the testimony of the experts is the same, and it is this fact which makes our task so encouraging. We have set ourselves to work to "strengthen such as do stand, to comfort and help the weak-hearted, and to raise up those who fall," and to have found out how this is to be done, is to have taken one step, at least, toward success.

CONTENTS

PART I. PUBLIC RELIEF.

PART II. PRIVATE CHARITY.

PART I. PUBLIC RELIEF.

CHAPTER I.

PUBLIC OUTDOOR RELIEF.

THEORY.

THE only justification for the spending of public money is, that the result is a public benefit, that is, that it is better for the whole mass of the people that the money should be spent.

It is not right to tax one part of the community for the benefit of another part; it is not right to take money by law from one man and give it to another, unless for the benefit of both. The public funds are always somebody's money; they are composed of the taxes which are very often hard to pay, or it would be safe to say, which are usually hard to pay; for the men to whom the payment of taxes is an unimportant item are the exceptions in every community, and pay but a very small proportion of the amount raised by taxation. The bulk comes from the many, who are struggling to keep or to obtain their own homes, and to whom a slight increase or decrease is a great matter.

Therefore, the policy of public poor relief, or the feeding and maintenance of one part of the people, by money taken by law from the rest, can be justified, only on the ground that it is better both for those who are so fed and maintained, and for those who supply the food and maintenance, that this should be done.

There are persons who argue that compulsory or public relief in all its forms, tends in the end to do harm, by diminishing prudence and industry, in consequence of removing, not only the most pressing incentive to those virtues (the fear of suffering and starvation), but also by diminishing the rewards of industry and forethought, which is necessarily done, when a part of what they gain is seized upon to feed indolence and improvidence. Those who argue thus, are undoubtedly right in the abstract, but they forget, apparently, that there are in every community, persons who cannot maintain themselves, and who have no friends upon whom they have a claim, and that it would not be well, even for others, that these should be driven to desperation by the absolute pressure of want; in this view, public relief is a benefit to the whole people, acting as a preventive of violence. Those who object to public relief in all its forms, also seem to forget that human pity is imperative, and that were there no final resort for those who cannot maintain themselves, nor assurance against their dying by starvation, it would be absolutely impossible to refuse food and money to all who asked for it. They would ask on the ground that they were starving, and the possibility that such might be the case would open every hand, and in this way a far greater temptation to idleness, improvidence and fraud would be afforded, than any public relief system could present, and a larger share of the earnings of hard-worked men and women would be absorbed by idleness and vice.

It will scarcely be denied by any one that, if possible, all the members of any civilized community must live. To live, they must be maintained by the produce of those members who work, and so create the means of living. The question is as to the way in which this produce shall be taken from those who create it, and given to those who can not create it. Shall it be done systematically, so that it will supply only those who actually can not create it, and thus reduce the amount to be taken to a minimum, or shall it be distributed by the producers themselves, who will be a prey to all who pretend that they can not create it? In other words, shall there or shall there not be public relief?

In Ireland, before the establishment of any poor-law, one cause of the suffering of the cottiers, as stated by Sir George Nichols, author of the History of the English, Scotch and Irish Poor-laws, was the extraordinary number of beggars, who invaded every cabin, and were maintained by those nearly as poor as themselves, and in every community the amount given to unknown and often unworthy beggars is undoubtedly a decided tax on industry, which would be increased almost indefinitely, were there no public and systematized means of relieving the poor. Public relief, then, appears to be not only a benefit to the whole community, but a necessity. The next point is as to the best form it can assume, and to decide upon this, it is necessary to define clearly the objects of public relief. They seem to be all included under the following heads :

1. To provide that no one shall starve, or shall suffer for the absolute physical necessaries of life.

2. To make this provision in such a way as shall do as little moral harm as possible, both to the recipient of relief and to the community at large.

3. To use every means to render the necessity for relief of short duration.

4. To take as small a sum from the tax-paying (that is the working) part of the community as is consistent with the accomplishment of the first three objects.

5. To convince the community that all these objects are attained, and that consequently, they

need not take upon themselves the provision of the necessaries of life for those who have no direct or personal claim upon them.

Such being the objects, how are they to be attained? What are the methods by which public relief may be wisely given—that is, by which a certain part of the people may be fed and maintained by the rest?

There are only two methods with which we need now to concern ourselves—these are outdoor relief and relief in a work-house or alms-house, or in other words, relief given to poor persons at their own homes (outside the doors of the work-house or alms-house) and relief administered inside of an institution, built and maintained at the public expense and controlled by public officials.

It would seem that, *a priori*, every argument was in favor of the first method—of out-door relief. Given, a community of which some of the members are to be fed and clothed at the cost of the rest, it would be said at once, that the right and simple way was to furnish to them, in their own homes, such relief as they required, and that in this way, all the objects aimed at would be attained.

1. They would be saved from starvation or suffering.

2. Neither they, nor any other person, would

suffer moral injury, because they, living in their own homes, would not be brought in close contact with any one else, either to corrupt or be corrupted —none of the natural relations, either of the family or the community, would be interrupted.

3. The relief would be of short duration, because, the need having passed, the relief would stop as a matter of course.

4. It would be much the cheapest method of giving relief, because all the expense incurred would be for absolute necessaries, food, fuel and clothing, and even this would be reduced to a minimum, because often all that would be required would be a small sum to supplement the means of living, which would be cut off were relief inside an institution to be substituted; while in the latter case, the cost of the building and of supervision would also have to be added.

5. The public would certainly be satisfied when assured that the wants of every poor person were supplied at their own homes; while on the other hand the public would certainly not be reconciled to the fact that, simply because a man was poor, therefore his home was to be broken up, and he and his family be sent into a work-house to become paupers.

These are the arguments on the side of out-door relief; arguments which, as arguments, are un-answerable.   Considered *a priori*, the decision would seem to be inevitably in favor of out-door relief. Fortunately, however, or unfortunately, considering the results of experiment, the effect on a community of out-door relief is not a field for *a priori* argument; not only in our own country have partial experiments in this direction been made, but in other countries, more especially in England, has the whole question been put to a practical test and proved to the very extreme of danger, the results being the exact opposite of what it seemed reasonable to expect.

About the end of the last century, the upper and middle classes of England, reasoning *a priori* (and influenced, undoubtedly, by the French Revolution) came to the conclusion that every man ought to be able to make a living for himself and his family, and that, if he could not make it, it should be furnished him; they not only came to this conclusion, but they acted upon it, and for about fifty years there was no man in England who, however idle, vicious or even dangerous he might be, could not obtain from the "Rates" (that is, the taxes on land) the means of supporting himself and his family of six, or ten, or twenty children and grandchildren.

Instead, however, of increased comfort and prosperity and of diminished suffering, the tide of poverty, most unaccountably, rose higher and higher, and the flood of pauperism seemed about to engulf not only the paupers themselves, but the whole population of England.

There was not only a constant failure of all the efforts to check pauperism and crime, but the anomaly was apparently presented that the very efforts intended to check them merely served to increase them.

Such a state of things could not fail to attract the attention of the statesmen and philanthropists of the time, and throughout this whole period (from 1790 to 1834) there are writings and reports of all kinds upon the subject, both from irresponsible persons and by commissions appointed by Parliament, all presenting the same picture of unmitigated woe and deep and growing degradation.

CHAPTER II.

PUBLIC OUTDOOR RELIEF PRACTICE IN ENGLAND.

As early as 1798, Malthus wrote :

"Fortunately for England a spirit of independence still remains among the peasantry. The poor laws are strongly calculated to eradicate this spirit. They have succeeded in part ; but had they succeeded as completely as might have been expected, their pernicious tendency would not have been so long concealed.

"Hard as it may appear in individual instances, dependent poverty ought to be held disgraceful. Such a stimulus seems to be absolutely necessary to promote the happiness of the great mass of mankind ; and every general attempt to weaken this stimulus, however benevolent its intention, will always defeat its own purpose. If men be induced to marry from the mere prospect of parish provision, they are not only unjustly tempted to bring unhappiness and dependence upon themselves and their children, but they are tempted without knowing it, to injure all in the same class with themselves.

"The parish laws of England appear to have contributed to raise the price of provisions, and to lower the real price of labor. They have therefore contributed to impoverish that class of people whose only possession is their labor. It is also difficult to suppose that they have not powerfully contributed to generate that carelessness and want of frugality, observable among the poor, so contrary to the disposition generally to be remarked among petty tradesmen and small farmers. The laboring poor, to use a common expression, seem always to live from hand to mouth. Their present wants employ their whole attention; and they seldom think of the future. Even when they have an opportunity of saving they seldom exercise it; but all that they earn beyond their present necessities goes, generally speaking, to the ale-house. The poor laws may therefore be said to diminish both the power and the will to save among the common people, and thus to weaken one of the strongest incentives to sobriety and industry, and consequently to happiness.   *   *   *   *

"The poor laws of England were undoubtedly instituted for the most benevolent purpose; but it is evident they have failed in attaining it. They certainly mitigate some cases of severe distress which might otherwise occur, though the state of the poor who are supported by parishes, considered in all its circumstances, is very miserable. But one of the principal objections to the system is, that for the assistance which some of the poor receive, in itself almost a doubtful blessing, the whole class of common people of England is subject to a set of grating, inconvenient, and tyrannical laws, totally inconsistent with the genuine spirit of the constitution.

"The whole business of settlements, even in its present amended state, is contradictory to all ideas of freedom. The parish persecution of men whose families are liable to become chargeable, and of poor women who are near lying in, is a most disgraceful and disgusting tryanny. And the obstructions continually occasioned in the market of labor by these laws have a constant tendency to add to the difficulties of those who are struggling to support themselves without assistance."

In 1817 a Parliamentary Committee, appointed
to inquire into the condition of the Poor, and pre-
sided over by Mr. Sturges Bourne, presented a
Report from which extracts are given below :

"A compulsory contribution for the indigent from the
funds originally accumulated from the labor and industry
of others could not fail in process of time, with the increase of population which it was calculated to foster, to
produce the unfortunate effect of abating those exertions
on the part of the laboring classes on which, according to
the nature of things, the happiness and welfare of mankind have been made to rest. By diminishing this natural impulse by which men are instigated to industry and
good conduct, by superseding the necessity of providing
in the season of health and vigor for the wants of sickness
and old age, and by making poverty and misery the conditions on which relief is to be obtained, your committee
can not but fear, from a reference to the increased numbers of the poor, and the increased and increasing amount
of the sums raised for their relief, that this system is perpetually encouraging and increasing the amount of misery it was designed to alleviate, creating at the same time
an unlimited demand on funds which it cannot augment ;
and as every system of relief founded on compulsory en-
actments must be divested of the character of benevolence, so it is without its beneficial effects; as it proceeds
from no impulse of charity, it creates no feeling of gratitude, and not unfrequently engenders dispositions and
habits calculated to separate rather than unite the interests of the higher and lower orders of the community;
even the obligations of natural affection are no longer
left to their own impulse, but the mutual support of the

nearest relations has been actually enjoined by a positive law, which the authority of magistrates is continually required to enforce.

" The progress of these evils, which are inherent in the system itself, appears to have been favored by the circumstances of modern times, by an extension of the law in practice, and by some deviations from its most important provisions. How much of the complaints which have been referred to your committee may be attributable to one cause or the other it is perhaps not easy to ascertain. The result, however, appears to have been highly prejudicial to the moral habits, and consequent happiness, of a great body of the people, who have been reduced to the degradation of a dependence upon parochial support, while the rest of the community, including the most industrious class, has been oppressed by a weight of contribution taken from those very means which would otherwise have been applied more beneficially to the supply of employment, and as the funds which each person can expend in labor are limited in proportion as the poor rate diminishes those funds, in the same proportion will the wages of labor be reduced to the immediate and direct prejudice of the laboring classes; the system thus producing the very necessity which it is created to relieve."

Still, however, the evils described, continued to grow, and in Feburary 1832, a Commission was appointed by the Crown and was directed to " make a diligent and full inquiry into the practical operation of the laws for the relief of the poor in England and Wales, and into the manner in which those laws are administered, and to report whether any and what alterations, amendments or improvements may be beneficially made in the said laws, or in the manner of administering them and how the same may be best carried into effect."

The following account of the powers and action of the Commissioners is taken from " The History of the English Poor Law," by Sir George Nichols :

"' They were empowered to appoint assistant or itinerant commissioners to visit the several districts both urban and rural, and report the practices which they found to prevail, so that the different modes in which relief was administered in different parts of the country, and the effects produced in each case, might become known, and serve as guides in framing any measure which the commissioners might deem it necessary to recommend. The assistants were appointed and instructed in the nature of the duties required from them with as little delay as possible, and queries were likewise extensively circulated throughout the country, the returns to which afforded much valuable information.

" The subject to be inquired into was, however, so large and complicated, that much time was unavoidably occupied in preparation, and in what may be called preliminary matters, producing no immediate result. But on the 19th of March, 1833, in compliance with a request to that effect, the commissioners presented to the government a volume of extracts, containing generally the substance of the information they had up to that time received, and which, although comprising only a small portion of the evidence in their possession, they declared it to be their belief, 'contained more information on the subject to which it relates, than had ever yet been afforded to the country.' The commissioners further remark that ' the most important and certainly the most painful part of its contents are the proof that the maladministration, which was supposed to be principally confined to some of the agricultural districts, appears to have spread over almost every part of the country, and into the manufacturing towns, the proof that actual intimidation, directed against those who are, or are supposed to be, unfavorable to profuse relief, is one of the most extensive sources of maladministration, and the proof that the evils though checked in some places by extraordinary energy and talent, is on the whole steadily and rapidly progressive.'

"This volume of extracts was distributed throughout the country, and produced a very marked effect on the public mind, the information it contained being admirably selected and arranged for the purpose. It was followed on the 20th of February in the succeeding year, by the full and very elaborate report of the commissioners, with an abridged supplement appended, and also accompanied by an appendix, of which the commissioners remark : ' The evidence contained in our appendix comes from every county and almost every town, and from a very large proportion of even the villages in England. It is derived from many thousand witnesses of every rank, and of every profession and employment—members of the two houses of Parliament, clergymen, country gentlemen, magistrates, farmers, manufacturers, shop-keepers, artisans and peasants, differing in every conceivable degree in education, habits and interests, and agreeing only in their practical experience as to the matters in question, in their general description both of the mode in which the laws for the relief of the poor are administered, and of the consequences which have already resulted from the administration, and in their anticipation of certain further consequences from its continuance.' The commissioners then declare their opinion that ' the amendment of those laws is perhaps the most urgent and the most important measure now remaining for the consideration of parliament,' and they express a hope that they shall facilitate that amendment ' by tendering the most extensive, and at the same time, the most consistent body of evidence that was ever brought to bear on a single subject.' The report is signed by the bishop of London, the bishop of Chester, Sturges Bourne, Nassau, W. Senior, Henry Bishop, Henry Gaivler, W. Coulson, James Trail and Edward Chadwick —names deserving to be held in grateful remembrance by all who love their country, and feel an interest in the welfare of the people."

I make no excuse for giving very copious extracts from the Report itself, for I consider that it is probably the most instructive historical document in existence which relates to pauperism.

The Commissioners give the following account of the gradual, growth of the practice of administering " Outdoor Relief."

" The history of the Poor Laws abounds with instances of a legislation which has been worse than unsuccessful, which has not merely failed in effecting its purposes, but has been active in producing effects which were directly opposed to them, has created whatever it was intended to prevent and fostered whatever it was intended to discourage.

"'One clause in the 9 Geo. I, was however efficient in promoting the objects of that Act—that which enabled parishes to purchase or hire, or unite in purchasing or hiring a workhouse, and to contract for the maintenance there of their poor, and enacted that any persons who should refuse to be lodged in such houses should not be entitled to receive collection or relief. An enactment which, while it was in operation, appears to have checked the increase of pauperism, and in many instances to have occasioned its positive diminution.'

"But towards the end of the last century, a period arrived when the accidents of the seasons and other causes occasioned a rise in the price of the necessaries of life. If things had been left to take their course, the consequences in England would have been what they were in Scotland, and what they were with us in those occupations, which, from their requiring skill, raise the workingman above the region of parish relief. Wages would have risen to meet the depreciation of money, and the laborer would have earned the same or nearly the same amount of raw produce, and a larger amount of manufactured commodities.

" But things were not left to take their own course. Unhappily no knowledge is so rare as the knowledge when to do nothing. It requires an acquaintance with general principles, a confidence in their truth, and a patience of the gradual process by which obstacles are steadily but slowly surmounted, which are among the last acquisitions of political science and experience. Under the 3 and 4 Will. and Mary, and 9 Geo. I., or under the 5 Eliz. c. 4, empowering the Justices to fix the rate of wages, it appeared that the existing difficulties might be instantly got rid of. The latter statute appeared to enable a forced rise of wages, the former statutes appeared to enable relief to be ordered if wages should remain insufficient. Each plan was proposed. Sir Frederick Eden's account of the mode in which the latter plan was adopted is so instructive that we will venture to quote it.

" 'Instead of an advance in wages proportioned to the increased demand for labor, the laborer has received a considerable part of that portion of his employer's capital which was destined for his maintenance in the form of poor's rate (the very worst that it could assume) instead of being paid it, as the fair, well-earned recompense of equivalent labor. This is a deplorable evil, which has fallen heavier on the poor than on the rich; and it has been considerably aggravated by the very injudicious steps which have been adopted for administering relief to those whom the pressure of the late scarcity had incapacitated from supporting themselves and families in the way to which they had been accustomed. Many instances might be adduced of the ill effects of the indiscriminating charity of individuals, and of the no less ill effects of the discriminating interference of magistrates and parish officers; but that I may not swell this work to too great a length, I shall content myself with offering a short statement (which was obligingly communicated to me by a gentleman who himself served the office of overseer in his own parish), of the proceedings which took place in a single county, for the relief of the poor last year.

" 'The very great price of the necessaries of life, but more particularly of bread-corn, during the whole of last year, produced extraordinary demands for parochial assistance. In many parishes in the county of Berks relief from the poor's rates was granted, not only to the infirm and impotent, but to the able-bodied and industrious, who had very few of them ever applied to the parish for relief, and then only during temporary illness or disability. There was no doubt but that the circumstances of the times required an increase in the income of the laborers in husbandry who in this country at least compose the most numerous body of those liable to want assistance from the parish. But there existed a difference of opinion respecting the mode of making such increase. In order to apply adequate remedy to the evil, a meeting of the magistrates for the county was held about Easter, 1795, when the following plans were submitted to their consideration:

" ' 1st. That the magistrates should fix the lowest price to be given for labor as they were empowered to do by 5 Eliz. c. 4; and secondly, that they should act with uniformity in the relief of the impotent and infirm poor, by a table of universal practice corresponding with the supposed necessities of each family. The first plan was rejected by a considerable majority, but the second was adopted.

" ' Had political relations not interfered, the demand for labor would have raised its price, not only in a ratio merely adequate to the wants of the laborer, but even beyond it ; and that price would have been advanced by the individual who employed him, instead of being a general tax on those who are liable to be rated, and who are not all employers of laborers. The capital which employs labor has increased ;   the demand of labor would consequently increase. It did increase, for the situation of the laboring poor in Berks was never better than during the last hard winter ; but they received these advanced wages in the way most prejudicial to their moral interests ; they received it as charity, as the extorted charity of others, and not as the result of their own well-exerted industry; and it was paid them not by their immediate employers, but by those who were in many instances, not the employers in any labor.'

"The clause of the 9th Geo. I, c. 7, prohibiting relief to those who refused to enter the workhouse was however an obstacle; to remove it the 36 Geo. 3d, c. 23 was passed. That act after reciting the clause in question, proceeds thus:

"'And whereas the said provision contained in the Act above-mentioned has been found to have been and to be inconvenient and oppressive, inasmuch as it often prevents an industrious poor person from receiving such occasional relief as is best suited to the peculiar case of such poor person; and inasmuch as in certain cases it holds out certain conditions of relief, injurious to the comfort, and domestic situation, and happiness of such poor persons.'

"And then repeals the clause forbidding relief to those who should refuse to enter the workhouse, and proceeds more directly to its object by the following provision: 'And be it further enacted, that it shall be lawful for any of his majesty's justice or justices of the peace of any county, city, town or place, usually acting in and for the district wherein the same shall be situated, at his or their proper discretion, to direct and order collection or relief to any industrious poor person; and he shall be entitled to ask and receive such relief, at his home or house in any parish, town, township or place, notwithstanding any contract, shall have been or shall be made, for lodging, keeping, maintaining and employing poor persons in a house for such purpose hired or purchased; and the overseers for such parish, town, township or place are required and directed to obey and perform such order for relief given by any justice or justices as aforesaid.'

" Those who are irritated by the pressure of the evils which allowance to the able-bodied has produced, and by the apprehension of the still greater evils which it may be expected to produce, are sometimes inclined to attribute the most childish folly, or the most profligate dishonesty to those who could aid in establishing such a system. But we must not judge them according to the knowledge which we have acquired in the dear-bought experience of forty years. It is clear that when the magistrates assembled at Speenhamland in 1795 'to settle the weekly income of the industrious poor' public opinion sanctioned their attempt. This is shown by the 36th Geo. 3d, c. 23, which was passed a few months after, and may be considered the great and fatal deviation from our previous policy. The 43d Elizabeth never contemplated as objects of relief industrious persons. It made no promises of comfort or happiness; it directed that those having no means, and using no daily trade of life to get their living by, should be set to work, and that the impotent should receive the necessary relief. These were unalluring offers —they held out nothing but work and necessary relief, and those only to the impotent, and to persons who must always form a small minority in any tolerably regulated society, that is persons having no property, and using no daily trade. The able-bodied industrious laborer was carefully excluded and relief therefore, as Mr. Pitt (in the speech introducing his Poor Bill in 1796) complained became a ground for opprobrium and contempt. They were precise offers:—the question whether a person using no trade had been set to work, or one unable to work had received necessary relief, were matters of fact. The engagements of the 43d Elizabeth, were perhaps dangerous engagements, but they were engagements which for 100 years were performed apparently without substantial injury to the morals and industry of the laborers, or to the general prosperity of the country. And whatever may be the objection in principle to the power given to the magistrates or assumed by them under the 3d and 4th Will. and Mary, and 9th Geo. I. it does not seem to have produced much practical evil while the 9th Geo. I. was in force. Parochial relief appears to have been given chiefly through the workhouse, and not to have been extended to many besides the impotent. The duty of the magistrates was tolerably plain ; if the applicant fell within the classes pointed out by the 43d Elizabeth as objects of relief, that is if he had no property, used no ordinary or daily trade to get his living by, or was lame, impotent, blind, or otherwise not able to work, he could direct him to be admitted into the workhouse, and if he was included in the first class, set to work by the parish officers ; or if included in the second class, supplied with necessary relief. Relief was considered a burden to the payers, and a degradation to the receivers (and to be marked as such by a badge), a remedy for unexpected calamity and a mitigation of the punishment inflicted by nature on extravagance and im-providence, *but no part of the ordinary fund for the support of labor.* Public opinion sanctioned the magistrate in a sparing exercise of his power, and he had, in fact, no motive for undue interference. The paupers were a small disreputable minority, whose resentment was not to be feared, and whose favor was of no value ; all other classes were anxious to diminish the number of appli-cants, and to reduce the expense of their maintenance.

"The 36th of Geo. 3d removed all these fences; it recognized as objects of relief, industrious persons, and enabled the magistrate, at his just and proper discretion, to order it to be given in a way which should not be injurious to their comfort, domestic situation and happiness. Mr. Pitt's bill went still further ; it admitted within the pale of pauperism, not only the industrious laborer, but the person with property, and enabled him when possessed of land, not only to retain it while an applicant for relief but to be supplied at the expense of the parish, with a cow. It is true that this bill was dropped, but as it was not an individual, but a government measure, it may be cited as evidence of the general feeling on the subject.

"When allowance to the able-bodied, in aid of their wages had once been introduced, when it had been found to be an expedient by which the expenditure in wages could be reduced and profits and rents could be raised, when the paupers became numerous in most districts, and in some districts formed the majority and even the large majority of the peasantry; when their clamors for allowance were favored by the farmers, and apparently justified by the rise in the price of the necessaries of life, who can be surprised if the magistrates were led, in some places to connive at, in others to sanction, and, in still more, to promote, a practice, the evil of which had not then been experienced, which seemed so plausible in itself, and which so many persons combined to favor? Who can wonder, that thus urged and encouraged, they should have fancied themselves entitled to settle the weekly income of the laborers ; and who can wonder at any amount of evil that has followed so preposterous an attempt?"

Under the head of "General Remarks on Outdoor Relief," the Commissioners write:

"We have dwelt at some length on out-door relief, because it appears to be the relief now most extensively given, and because it appears to contain in itself the elements of an almost indefinite extension; of an extension, in short, which may ultimately absorb the whole fund out of which it arises. Among the elements of extension are the constantly diminishing reluctance to claim an apparent benefit, the receipt of which imposes no sacrifice, except a sensation of shame, quickly obliterated by habit, even if not prevented by example; the difficulty often amounting to impossibility, on the part of those who administer and award relief, of ascertaining whether any and what necessity for it exists; and the existence in many cases of positive motives on their parts to grant it when unnecessary, or themselves to create the necessity. The first and third of these sources of mal-administration are common to the towns and to the country; the second, the difficulty of ascertaining the wants of the applicants, operates most strongly in the large towns.

"From the preceding evidence it will be seen how zealous must be the agency, and how intense the vigilance, to prevent fraudulent claims crowding in under such a system of relief. But it would require still greater vigilance to prevent the bona fide claimants degenerating into impostors; and it is an aphorism amongst the active parish officers that 'cases which are good to-day are bad to-morrow, unless they are incessantly watched.' A person obtains relief on the grounds of sickness; when he has become capable of returning to moderate work he is tempted by the enjoyment of subsistence without labor, to conceal his convalescence, and fraudulently extend the period of relief. When it really depends upon the receivers whether the relief shall cease with its occasion, it is too much to expect of their virtue that they shall in any considerable number of instances, voluntarily forego the pension."

The Commissioners describe the effects of outdoor relief on " Laborers actually relieved," and " Not actually relieved."

" It gives him (the pauper) also, strange as it may appear, a sort of independence. He need not bestir himself to seek work; he need not study to please his master; he need not put any restraint upon his temper; he need not ask relief as a favor. He has all a slave's security for subsistence without his liability to punishment. As a single man indeed, his income does not exceed a bare subsistence; but he has only to marry, and it increases. Even then it is unequal to the support of a family; but it rises on the birth of every child. If his family is numerous the parish becomes his principal paymaster; for small as the usual allowance of 2 s. a head may be, yet, when there are more than three children, it generally exceeds the average wages given in a pauperized district. A man with a wife and six children, entitled according to the scale, to have his wages made up to 16 s. a week, in a parish where the wages paid by individuals do not exceed 10 or 12 s. is almost an irresponsible being. All the other classes of society are exposed to the vicissitudes of hope and fear; he alone has nothing to lose or gain."

" In Coggeshall, Essex," says Mr. Magendie, "weekly wages are 8 s. but by piece-work a good laborer may earn 10 s. Now consider the case of laborers with four children, for the subsistence of which family (according to the Chelmsford scale, which is the law of that district,) 11 s. and 6 d. is required. Of this sum the good laborer earns 10 s., and receives from the parish 1 s. 6 d. The inferior laborer earns 8 s., and receives from the parish 3 s. 6 d. The man who does not work, and whom no one will employ, receives the whole from the parish.

"Other classes of society are restrained from misconduct by fear of the evils which may result to their families. Parochial legislation rejects this sanction. In Barnard Castle, in Northumberland, Mr. Wilson states that if any remonstrance is made on account of the applicant's bad character the reply of the magistrate commonly is 'the children must not suffer for it.'

"The answer given by the magistrates when a man's bad conduct is urged by the overseer against his relief is, 'We can not help that; his wife and family are not to suffer because the man has done wrong.'

"Too frequently petty thieving, drunkenness or impertinence to a master throw able-bodied laborers, perhaps with large families, on the parish funds, when relief is demanded as a right, and if refused, enforced by a magistrate's order, without reference to the cause which has produced his distress, viz.; his own misconduct, which remains as a barrier to his obtaining any fresh situation, and leaves him a dead weight upon the honesty and industry of his parish.

"It appears to the pauper that the government has undertaken to repeal, in his favor, the ordinary laws of nature; to enact that the children shall not suffer for the misconduct of their parents—the wife for that of the husband, or the husband for that of the wife ; that no one shall lose the means of comfortable subsistence, whatever be his indolence, prodigality or vice; in short, that the penalty, which, after all must be paid by some one for idleness and improvidence is to fall, not on the guilty person or his family, but on the proprietors of the lands and houses encumbered by his settlements. Can we wonder if the uneducated are seduced into approving a system which aims its allurements at all the weakest parts of our nature, which offers marriage to the young, security to the anxious, ease to the lazy, and impunity to the profligate?

" We have seen that one of the objects attempted by the present administration of the Poor Law is to repeal *pro tanto* that law of nature by which the effects of each man's improvidence or misconduct are borne by himself and his family. The effect of that attempt has been to repeal *pro tanto* the law by which each man and his family enjoy the benefit of his own prudence and virtue. In abolishing punishment we equally abolish reward. Under the operation of the scale system—the system which directs the overseer to *regulate* the income of the laborers according to their families—idleness, improvidence and extravagance occasion no loss, and consequently diligence and economy can afford no gain. But to say merely that these virtues afford no gain is an inadequate expression; they are often the causes of absolute loss. We have seen that in many places, the income derived from the parish for easy or nominal work, or, as it is most significantly termed " in lieu of labor," *actually exceeds* that of the independent laborer; and even in those cases in which the relief money only equals, or nearly approaches the average rate of wages, it is often better worth having, as the pauper requires less expensive diet and clothing than the hard-working man. In such places a man who does not possess either some property or an amount of skill which will ensure to him more than the average rate of wages, is of course a loser by preserving his independence. Even if he have some property he is a loser, unless the aggregate of the income which it affords and of his wages equal what he would receive as a pauper. It appears accordingly that when a parish has become pauperized, the laborers are not only prodigal of their earnings, not only avoid accumulation, but even dispose of and waste in debauchery as soon as their families entitle them to allowance, any small property which may have devolved on them, or which they may have saved in happier times. Self-respect, however, is not yet so utterly destroyed among the English peasantry as to make this universal.

"But though the injustice perpetrated on the man who struggles, as far as he can struggle, against the oppression of the system, who refuses as far as he can refuse, to be its accomplice, is at first sight the most revolting; the severest sufferers are those who have become callous to their own degradation, who value parish support as their privilege, and demand it as their right, and complain only that it is limited in amount, or that some sort of labor or confinement is exacted in return. No man's principles can be corrupted without injury to society in general; but the person most injured is the person whose principles have been corrupted. The constant war which the pauper has to wage with all who employ or pay him, is destructive to his honesty and his temper; as his subsistence does not depend upon his exertions, he loses all that sweetens labor, its association with reward, and gets through his work, such as it is, with the reluctance of a slave. His pay, earned by importunity or fraud, or even violence, is not husbanded with the carefulness which would be given to the results of industry, but wasted in the intemperance to which his ample leisure invites him. The ground on which relief is ordered to the idle and dissolute is, that the wife and family must not suffer for the vices of the head of the family; but as that relief is almost always given into the hands of the vicious husband or parent, this excuse is obviously absurd. It appears from the evidence that the great supporters of the beer-shops are the paupers. 'Wherever,' says Mr. Lawrence, of Henfield, 'the laborers are unemployed, the beer-shops of the parish are frequented by them.' And it is a striking fact that in Cholesbury, where, out of 139 individuals, only 35 persons, of all ages, including the clergyman and his family, are supported by their own exertions there are two public houses."

" Hundreds of instances," says Mr. Okeden, "came under my observation, in which the overseers knew that the wages and parish allowance were spent in two nights at the beer-houses, which ought to have been the week's subsistence for the whole family. Still no steps are taken, the scale is referred to, and acted on, and the parish actually supports and pays for the drunken excesses of the laborers. The character and habits of the laborer have, by this scale system, been completely changed. Industry fails, moral character is annihilated, and the poor man of twenty years ago, who tried to earn his money and was thankful for it, is now converted into an insolent, discontented, surly, thoughtless pauper, who talks of right and income, and who will soon fight for these supposed rights and income, unless some step is taken to arrest his progress to open violence. Some rude efforts he may, at first, make to shake off his state of servitude; but he finally yields to the temptations of the pay-table

and the scale, feels his bondage, puts off his generous
feeling of industry, and gratitude, and independence, and

To suit
His manner with his fate, puts on the brute."

" I can decidedly state as the result of my experience
that when once a family has received relief, it is to be expected that their descendants, for some generations, will
receive it also.

" The change made in the character and habits of the
poor, by once receiving parochial relief, is quite remarkable ; they are demoralized ever afterwards.

" I state it confidently, as the result of my experience,
that if once a young lad gets a pair of shoes given him
by the parish he never afterwards lays by sufficient to
buy a pair ; so if we give to the fathers or mothers of
children clothing or other assistance they invariably apply again and again.

" The regular applicants for relief are generally of one
family ; the disease is hereditary, and when once a family
has applied for relief, they are pressed down forever.

" Whether in work or out of work when they once became paupers, it can only be by a sort of miracle that
they can be broken off. They have no care, no thought,
no solicitude, on account of the future, except the old
musty rent-roll of receipts or an old dirty indenture of
apprenticeship, which are handed down from father to
son with as much care as deeds of freehold property, and
by which they pride themselves in the clear claim to the
parish money and the workhouse. All the tricks and
deceptions of which man is capable are resorted to ; the
vilest and most barefaced falsehoods are uttered, and the
worst characteristics of human nature are called into ex-

ercise for the purpose of exciting a favorable feeling in their behalf ; *their children are eye and ear witnesses to all this.* The child remembers his father's actions, and the hereditary pauper increases his ranks, by instruction as well as by example. Their numbers will, as a matter of course, still increase, while these laws exist in their present form."

The effect of Out door Relief in lowering wages is thus described :

" Ribbon-weaving is carried on to a great extent in all the villages around Coventry. Work is given out by the manufacturers to persons who are termed undertakers, who contract for it at a certain price, and the amount of their profit depends upon the rate at which they can procure labor ; they consequently seek it at the lowest possible price, and for this purpose it is said they often employ persons who are dependent on the county parishes, which of necessity, if done to any extent, must affect the rate of wages in the trade as much as if the competition arose in a foreign country.

" In the reply of the vestry clerk of Birmingham, he states that relief is given occasionally according to the number of children, but not given to eke out the wages of able-bodied persons *wholly* employed.

" Upon inquiring the meaning of the words *not wholly employed,* it was explained to refer to those persons whose masters had certified that they only enabled them to earn a half of the average rate of wages in any branch of manufacture. On this subject Mr. Lewis, the Governor of the workhouse at Erdington, who has the manangement of the poor at Aston, the immediate adjoining parish to Birmingham, and now included within the Borough, stated that he was in a manufacturing house for fifteen years at Birmingham, and that he is well acquainted with the practices of different masters, and that from his own knowledge he could state that what are called small masters in this town, *i. e.*, those employing one or two journeymen, and who also work for some of the other masters, were in the constant habit of employing men who were receiving allowances from the parish, and that many in consequence were able to undersell other masters who were paying the full wages themselves.

"The practice of paying the wages of manufacturers out of the rate is strongly illustrated in the case of Collumpton, at a short distance from Tiverton, where the weaving of serge and cloth is carried on by two manufacturers on whose employment many of the poor in that town have chiefly depended for support; one of these manufacturers, however, receives at present regular annual payments from the parishes in the neighborhood to employ their paupers, the sums paid being less than the cost of their support by the parishes. The same system is not adopted by the parish of Collumpton ; the result, therefore, with regard to the poor at large is not to diminish the amount of pauperism, but to change its locality; for the first effect of such a measure was to increase the number of persons unemployed at Collumpton, and consequently to reduce wages. It was operating also with injustice to the other manufacturer.

"On conversing with a manufacturer at Tewkesbury, I found that he regretted the great fall in wages, but said that as a capitalist he had no choice between reducing the wages of his men and giving up his business, and that if a certain proportion of the operatives were obliged to take lower wages, the wages of the rest must also fall, since otherwise the master who employed those at reduced wages would get possession of the market. He said that he could always calculate out of a given number of workmen what proportion working at low wages would bring down the rest; and that if any circumstance caused a fall in one district, wages must fall in all other districts producing the same article. He admitted that this would equally be the case, if the operatives in any number, were relieved by the parish.

"Stockings are made in all the neighboring parishes in a circle around Nottingham of twenty or more miles in diameter, in the cottages of the journeymen, who rent frames at 1 s. per week each, which they hire from a capitalist, who possesses, perhaps, several hundred, and the capitalist gives the operative work to do, and pays him wages. The operative in whatever parish he may be, is informed that his wages must be lowered, and in consequence applies to the parish; his master in Nottingham furnishes him with a certificate that he is only receiving (suppose) 6 s. a week; and thus the parishes were induced to allow him 4 s. or 5 s.

"Mr. Chaddick, the former overseer of Basford, which is a few miles from Nottingham, told me that this system was universal, and went into a calculation, proving that by means of it master manufacturers were enabled to sell stockings at a profit, though the selling price did not cover the prime cost, if the parochial addition to the wages paid by the master was to be taken as an element of the prime cost, as it undoubtedly ought to be.

"At Southwell, I heard of instances in which the master manufacturer had combined with his men to give them false certificates of the amount of their wages, so that they might claim a larger sum from the parish.

" Whole branches of manufacture may thus follow the course not of coal mines or of streams, but of pauperism ; may flourish like the funguses that spring from corruption in consequence of the abuses which are ruining all other interests of the places in which they are established, and cease to exist in the better administered districts in consequence of that better administration."

Mr. Henry Morley in Derbyshire says :

" When I was overseer I refused to relieve able-bodied men working for other people, considering that, by relieving them I was injuring the respectable part of the poor (I mean those just above pauperism) by running down their wages. I found that some of the children in the workhouse were put out to the cotton and silk mills, and because they were workhouse children, the manufacturers paid them less wages than were given to the children of independent work-people, who, on applying for employment for their children at 2 s. a week, were told 'I only give that girl who is older and bigger 1 s. 6 d.;' I determined therefore to take them away from the mills, and that they should do something, or even nothing in the house rather than injure the deserving poor. I am certain that for every 5 s. loss that the parish sustained by this conduct is gained £5 by assisting the respectable poor and by preventing them from requiring parish relief."

In the introduction to that part of their Report which treats of "Remedial Measures" the Commissioners say :

" It may be assumed that in the administration of relief, the public is warranted in imposing such conditions on the individual relieved, as are conducive to the benefit either of the individual himself, or of the country at large at whose expense he is to be relieved.

"The first and most essential of all conditions, a principle which we find universally admitted, even by those whose practice is at variance with it, is, that his situation on the whole shall not be made really or apparently so eligible as the situation of the independent laborer of the lowest class. Throughout the evidence it is shown that in proportion as the condition of any pauper class is elevated above the condition of independent laborers, the condition of the independent class is depressed; their industry is impaired, their employment becomes unsteady, and its remuneration in wages becomes diminished. Such persons, therefore, are under the strongest inducements to quit the less eligible class of laborers, and enter the more eligible class of paupers. The converse is the effect when the pauper class is placed in its proper position below the condition of the independent laborer. Every penny bestowed that tends to render the condition of the pauper more eligible than that of the independent laborer is a bounty on indolence and vice. We have found that as the poor rates are at present administered, they operate as bounties of this description, to the amount of several millions annually.

"The standard, therefore, to which reference must be made in fixing the condition of those who are to be maintained by the public, is the condition of those who are maintained by their own exertions. But the evidence shows how loosely and imperfectly the situation of the independent laborer has been inquired into, and how little is really known of it by those who award or distribute relief. It shows also that so little has their situation been made a standard for the supply of commodities, that the diet of the workhouse almost always exceeds that of the cottage, and the diet of the jail is generally more profuse than even that of the workhouse. It shows also that this standard has been so little referred to in the exaction of labor, that commonly the work required from the pauper is inferior to that performed by the laborers and servants of those who have prescribed it; so much so generally inferior as to create a prevalent notion among the agricultural paupers that they have a right to be exempted from the amount of work which is performed and indeed sought for by the independent laborer.

"But it will be seen that the process of depauperizing the able-bodied is, in its ultimate effects, a process which elevates the condition of the great mass of society.

"Before the experiment was made it might fairly have been anticipated that the discontinuance of parochial allowance would effect little or no improvement in wages unless a similar change were made in the neighboring parishes. When a considerable proportion of the laborers who had been entirely dependent upon the parish were driven to rely on their own industry, it might have been anticipated that the wages of the entire body of laborers within the parish would have been injuriously affected by their competition, and this certainly would have been the case if they had added nothing to the fund out of which their wages came. That fund is, in fact, periodically consumed and reproduced by the laborer, assisted by the land and the farmer's capital, and, all other things remaining the same, the amount of that fund, and consequently his share of it, or, in other words, the amount of his wages, depends on his industry and skill. If all the laborers in a parish cease to work they no longer produce any fund for their own subsistence, and must either starve or be supported, as they were at Cholesbury, by rates in aid. A single man who has no property and is supported without working bears the same relation to the laborers who do work as the parishioners of Cholesbury bore to the neighboring parishes. He is supported by a sort of rate in aid on their industry. His conversion from a pauper, wholly or partially supported by the labor of others, into an independendent laborer producing his own subsistence, and in addition to that a profit to his employer, so far from injuring his fellow workmen, produces on them the same effects as the enabling the inhabitants of Cholesbury to support themselves has produced on the parishes which had to supply them with rates in aid. This has been perceived by some of our witnesses. A farmer of considerable intelligence who had resided in Cookham, and observed the effects of the change in that parish, declared his conviction that if such a change could be generally introduced, the money saved in the poor's rate would almost immediately be paid in wages. The withdrawal of relief in aid of wages appears to be succeeded by effects in the following order:—First, the laborer becomes more steady and diligent; next, the more efficient laborer makes the return to the farmer's capital larger, and the consequent increase of the fund for the employment of labor enables and induces the capitalist to give better wages."

After describing the condition of the few parishes where, previous to their inquiry, outdoor relief had been cut off and paupers relieved only in a workhouse, the Commissioners say :

" From the above evidence it appears that wherever the

principle which we have thus stated has been carried into effect either wholly or partially, its introduction has been beneficial to the class for whose benefit the Poor Laws exist. We have seen that in every instance in which the able-bodied laborers have been rendered independent of partial relief, or of relief otherwise than in a well regulated workhouse :

1. Their industry has been restored and improved.

2. Frugal habits have been created or strengthened.

3. The permanent demand for their labor has increased.

4. And the increase has been such that their wages, so far from being depressed by the increased amount of labor in the market, have in general advanced.

5. The number of improvident and wretched marriages has diminished.

6. Their discontent has been abated, and their moral and social condition in every way improved."

The Commissioners recommend the total abolition of out-door relief, and then proceed :

"One objection we will answer immediately, and that is, that the whole or a large proportion of the present paupers must become inmates of the workhouse. One of the most encouraging of the results of our inquiry is the degree in which the existing pauperism arises from fraud, indolence or improvidence. If it had been principally the result of unavoidable distress we must have inferred the existence of an organic disease, which, without rendering the remedy less necessary, would have fearfully augmented its difficulty. But when we consider how strong are the motives to claim public assistance, and how ready are the means of obtaining it, independently of real necessity, we are surprised, not at the number of paupers,

but at the number of those who have escaped the conta-
gion. A person who attributes pauperism to the inability
to procure employment, will doubt the efficiency of the
means by which we propose to remove it, tried as they
have been and successful as they have always proved.

"In several of the depauperized parishes, the erection
of workhouses, and other remedial measures, were strongly
and sincerely opposed on similar grounds. In answer to
all objections founded on the supposition that the present
number of able-bodied paupers will remain permanently
chargeable, we refer to the evidence which shows the general causes of pauperism, and to the effects produced by
administration on a correct principle, as guaranteeing the
effects to be anticipated from the general application of
measures which have been tried by so many experiments.
But we cannot expect that such evidence will satisfy the
minds of those who sincerely disbelieve the possibility of
a class of laborers subsisting without rates in aid of wages;
and we have found numbers who have sincerely disbe-
lieved that possibility notwithstanding they have had daily
presented to their observation the fact, that laborers of
the same class, and otherwise no better circumstanced, do
live well without such allowances; still less can we expect
that such evidence will abate the clamors of those who
have a direct interest in the abuses which they defend
under the mask of benevolence.

"Such persons will no doubt avail themselves of the
mischievous ambiguity of the word *poor*, and treat all
diminution of the expenditure for the relief of the poor
as so much taken from the laboring classes, as if those
classes were naturally pensioners on the charity of their
superiors, and relief, not wages, were the proper fund for
their support; as if the independent laborers themselves

were not, directly or indirectly, losers by all expenditures
on paupers; as if those who would be raised from pauperism to independence would not be the greatest gain-
ers by the change; as if, to use the expression of one of
the witnesses we have quoted, 'the meat of industry were
worse than the bread of idleness.'

"To permit outdoor relief as an exception would be to
permit it as a rule. The construction which has been put
on the 59th George 3d., shows that every case would be
considered a case of emergency, and under provisions
directing that the able-bodied shall be relieved only in
the work house, but allowing relief in money to be continued to the sick, we must be prepared to find allowances
continued to many of the able-bodied as belonging to the
excepted class."

The Report of the Commissioners from which
the above extracts are taken was accompanied by
a Bill, entitled: "The 4th and 5th William IV.
Cap. 76, for the Amendment and Better Administration of the Laws relating to the Poor in England and Wales." In the course of his speech in
Parliament, moving its adoption, Lord Brougham,
then Lord Chancellor, spoke in part as follows:

"First, then, we have a constant, and I may say almost
a regular proof, in every part of the country, in districts
agricultural, manufacturing, and even commercial, and
whether the people are superabundant or scarce, increasing, stationary or diminishing in numbers, that able-bodied
men prefer a small sum in idleness, to a larger sum in
wages, attended with the condition of earning those
wages by labor. We have in one place a young man say-

ing: 'I have 3 s. 6 d. a week from the parish.   I do no work.   I have no need to labor; I would rather have my 3 s. 6 d. without working than toil to get 10 s. or 12 s. a week.'   This is not a single instance.   But are these persons only idle?   Are they really doing nothing?   Do they receive 3 s. 6 d. and remain inactive?   Do they work no mischief?   My Lords, it is idle in me to put such questions.   These persons are making the parish pay 3 s. 6 d. a week out of the honest laborer's hard earnings, to maintain the constant promoters of crime, the greatest workers of mischief in the country; men, who, when they happen not to be ring-leaders, are the ready accomplices and followers in every depredation, every outrage that is perpetrated in their neighborhood.   But these facts are not confined to agricultural districts, or inland places, or to lazy rustics.   Look to the hardy sailor who never used to know what danger was; look to the very boatmen of the Kentish coast—they who formerly would rush to a wreck without looking to the waves any more than to the reward—who would encounter the most appalling perils to save a life with as much alacrity as they would dance around a May-pole, or run a cargo of smuggled goods in the midst of a tempest, or in the teeth of the preventive service; these men, who, if you had ever said, in former times, 'Surely you do not mean to launch your boat at this tempestuous time of year?' would answer by instinct, 'Time of year! We take no account of season— by our boats we live; from the sea in winter as in summer, we must seek our sustenance; fair weather or foul, our vessels must be afloat, else how could we keep our families from the parish?'   No such answer will you get now.   The same spirit of honest and daring independence inflames them no more.   'We have 12*s.* a week from

the parish,' say the Kentish sailors; 'we will go out no
longer in winter—we will wait for summer and fair weather
—we will live at home the while, for the parish fund provides us.' Comment upon such facts is superfluous.
But the same classes now assume that they who live upon
the parish have a right not only to work as little as the
independent laborer, but not to work so hard. They have
in many places distinctly set up this claim; and in one or
two instances appeals have actually been made by the
pauper against the overseers, upon the ground that the
latter had attempted, as they say, 'A thing till then unknown in these parishes to make the paupers work the
same number of hours in the day as the independent
laborers, who receive no parochial assistance.' These are
things which almost force incredulity; but when we see
them proved by evidence which admits of no doubt, belief is extorted from us. Then it is needless to say that
the parish pauper regards himself independent of fair
weather or foul, of bad health or good, of the full harvest
or scanty crop, of all the calamities to which the rest of
mankind are subject. Again: All shame of begging is
utterly banished—the pauper glories in his dependence—
if, indeed, he does not consider the land as his own and
its nominal proprietor as his steward. Nay, instances are
to be found of the shame, being by a marvelous perver-
sion of feeling, turned the other way; and the solitary
exception to the rule of parish relief under which a whole
hamlet lived, 'being shamed,' as a female said, 'out of
her singularity and forced by her neighbors to take the
dole like themselves!' But, for all this I do not blame
the pauper; I blame the bad law and its worse administration which have made him a worthless member of
society. The law of nature says that a man shall support

his child—that the child shall support his aged and infirm parent—and that near relations shall succor one another in distress. But our law speaks another language, saying to the parent: 'Take no trouble of providing for your child,'—to the child, 'Undertake not the load of supporting your parent—throw away none of your money on your unfortunate brother and sister—all these duties the public will take on itself.' It is, in truth, one of the most painful and disgusting features of this law, that it has so far altered the nature of men. It is now a common thing to hear the father say: 'If you only allow me so many shillings a week for my children, I will drive them from my doors, and deny them the shelter of my roof;' and it is not unusual to hear the child say: 'If you do not allow my aged mother more I shall take her out of my house and lay her in the street or at the overseer's door.'"

Sir George Nichols, in his "History of the English Poor Law," still speaking of this period (1830–4), and of the work of the Commissioners, writes as follows:

"It is worthy of especial notice, that in the counties where the largest amount of relief was afforded under the Poor Law, the greatest number of riots and rick burnings occurred in the years 1830 and 1831, thus seeming to establish a close relationship between the one and the other, in the nature of cause and effect. The commission of inquiry adopt this view, which they support by citing the instances. The commissioners remark that 'the counties in which the expenditure is large are those in which the industry and skill of the laborers are passing away, the con-

nection between master and servant has become precari-
ous, the unmarried are defrauded of their fair earnings,
riots and incendiarisms have prevailed.   The three counties in which it is comparatively small, are those in which
scarcely any instance of fire or tumult appears to have
occurred, in which mutual attachment exists between the
workman and his employer, in which wages depend not on
marriages but on ability, and the diligence and skill of
the laborers are unimpaired and increased.'

"The state of feeling which prevailed in the southern
agricultural counties toward the end of 1830, has been
thus described: 'The farmers and their families had no
comfort in their lives. All day they looked with unavoidable suspicion upon the most ill-conditioned of their
neighbors, and on every stranger who came into the
parish. All night they were wakeful, either acting as
patrols, or looking out toward the stack-yards, or listening
for the rumble of the fire-engine. If a man weary with
patroling for three or four nights hoped for a night's sleep,
and went the last thing to his rick-yard, and explored
every corner, and visited every shed on his premises, he
might find his chamber illuminated by his burning ricks
by the time he could get up stairs. This was naturally
a time for malicious or encroaching persons to send
threatening letters, and for foolish jesters to play off
practical jokes, and for timid persons to take needless
alarms, and for all the discontented to make the most of
their grievances, and a dreary season of apprehension
indeed it was. The military were harassed with fruitless
marches, their nightly path lighted by fires from behind,
whichever way they turned. Large rewards were offered
—£500 for a single conviction, and these rewards were
believed to have been now and then obtained by the

instigators, while the poor tools were given over to destruction.'

"Such was the state of a large portion of the agricultural districts in the south of England, a very short time before the passing of the Poor Law Amendment Act. There may have been, and probably were, various causes in operation of longer or shorter standing, to bring about such a state of things; but it can hardly be doubted that the maladministration of the Poor Laws was one of them, if it were not, as indeed seems most likely, the principal cause. Wherever the allowance system prevailed in any form, or to any extent, a part of the laborer's wages, greater or less, according to the circumstances of the district, would be dealt out to him in the shape of parish relief, and there would be a constant struggle between him and the parish authorities (that is, the farmers and the employers of labor) on their part to give as little as possible, and on the laborer's part to obtain as much as possible out of that fund to which he had been trained up to believe his right was as good as theirs. Can we wonder, then, that an ill-feeling should exist between parties so situated, that the roundsman, or the laborer, under the allowance system should look upon his employer as a tyrant, and an oppressor who withheld from him and his family an allowance to which they had a right, and that he and they should regard such employer with feelings of hatred and revenge, for the manifestation of which an opportunity only was required. Now incendiarism afforded this opportunity, and also the simplest and safest means of gratifying revengeful feelings, however engendered, or from whatever cause arising, and we see the consequences painted with great force and truth in the extracts given above."

Under the Act referred to, Poor Law Commissioners were appointed, and the following extracts from Sir George Nichols's History show the character of their first Annual Report, dated August 8, 1835 :

"Anxious attention had been directed to the effect of the change upon the working classes, more especially upon those who had been accustomed to the allowance system, and inquiries were made as to the subsequent condition of the laborers whose allowance had been discontinued, and who notwithstanding, refused to accept relief in a workhouse. It was found that these persons generally obtained independent employment without quitting their parishes, and the commissioners cite the example of the Faringdon nnion, in which all out-door relief was discontinued, and relief in the workhouse was offered to 240 able-bodied laborers, and more than about twenty of whom entered the house, and not one-half of these remained there more than a few days, 'the diet in the workhouse being at the same time high, as compared with the diet of large classes of independent laborers.' It is further stated that all the more recent reports from the dispauperized districts represent the wages as being improved, and that the amounts paid are greater than in the adjacent pauperized parishes.

" The commissioners declare that they see nothing to prevent the extension of the union system to the less pauperized districts not yet visited, its advantages being universally applicable, and they further state their intention of revising their orders and arrangements from time to time 'with a view to a closer and ultimately to a complete adoption of the workhouse system, and the extinc-

tion of all out-door relief to the able-bodied.' In con-
cluding their report, the commissioners observe, that they
are sustained in their labors by the conviction that the
act which they had to administer will fulfill the beneficent
intentions of the legislature, and will conduce to elevate
the moral and social condition of the laboring classes and
promote the welfare of all."

Unhappily for England, the wise suggestions of
the Poor Law Commissioners have never been
carried out, and the country still groans under a
heavy burden of pauperism, due in great measure,
as experts believe, to the unwise administration of
Public Out-door Relief.

The testimony of two authorities since 1835 will
suffice :

From First Report of the Local Government Board,
    1871–72.   Presented to both Houses of Parliament by
    command of Her Majesty :

    Extracts from Circular Letter to Guardians, 1871.
    "It has been shown that in numerous instances the
Guardians disregard the advantages which result not only
to the rate-payers but to the poor themselves from the
offer of in-door in preference to out-door relief. A certainty of obtaining out-door relief in his own home when-
ever he may ask for it extinguishes in the mind of
the laborer all motive for husbanding his resources, and
induces him to rely exclusively upon the rates instead of
upon his own savings for such relief as he may require.
It removes every incentive to self-reliance and prudent
forethought on his part, and induces him, moreover,

to apply for relief on occasions when the circumstances are not such as to render him absolutely in need of it.

"For instance, in the Amersham Union, Buckinghamshire, during the winter of 1869, 212 persons applied for relief, all of whom received orders for the workhouse, which not one of the applicants, however, entered. In the Wellington Union (Salop), in-door relief was ordered by the Guardians during the last half year ended midsummer, 1871, to 322 individuals, of whom six only entered the workhouse, and of 99 families to whom indoor relief was offered in the same union during the three years preceding Christmas last, the same number of six alone availed themselves of such relief. The Guardians of the Uxbridge Union gave, on the 5th of January last, orders for the workhouse to 269 persons ; of that number twelve only entered the house, of whom seven discharged themselves on the same day, leaving five only who availed themself of the proposed relief. The Poor Law Inspector of the district subsequently ascertained that not one of the persons who applied for relief, and to whom indoor relief had been offered, had again asked for assistance. Some Guardians also are inclined to imagine that out-door relief is more economical than in-door, because one individual or family costs more in the workhouse than the amount of out-door relief which would be given in the particular case out of it.

"This no doubt may be so in an individual case, but the grant of out-door relief multiplies so largely the number of applicants that if relief were afforded to all, the cost of such relief would greatly exceed that of maintaining in the workhouse such of the applicants as would be willing to enter it."

The second extract is from a paper by Sir Charles

Trevelyan (a high authority), written only a few months ago. He says:

"By far the most demoralizing influence of our time and country is poor law out-door relief, which is an abnormal departure from the original institution.

. . . .

"Upon in-door relief there is a natural check. Nobody asks for it as a favor, and there is a strong presumption that everybody who accepts it is really in need of it.

"Upon out-door relief, on the contrary, there is no self-acting check, for it is a pension, comfortably enjoyed at home in addition to every other advantage and source of income, and everybody is glad to have it. The more a man saves, the less he gets of out-door relief ; if by industry and self-denial he entirely provides for himself, he gets nothing ; if he spends everything at the public house or in any other kind of self-indulgence, he entitles himself to the full measure of out-relief at the expense of the honest and self-denying. It is useless to exhort to industry and thrift, while in practice we hold out this lifelong encouragement to idleness and prodigality."

CHAPTER III.

Public Out-door Relief.

PRACTICE IN EUROPE AND THE UNITED STATES.

In 1874 an inquiry was made by the British Government concerning Poor Laws in foreign countries, and the results were published by the Local Government Board. The following are extracts from this report :

* " Attention is called by Sir Henry Barron to a very remarkable peculiarity in the pauperism and expenditures of the several provinces [of Belgium]. It appears that while the pauperism of the whole kingdom in the year 1868 was 11.3 per cent., that of the province of Luxemburg was only 2.2. In a subsequent part of the report Luxemburg appears to have 'next to no revenue for the poor, *yet no complaints of dearth and distress ever come from that quarter.*' "

" As to the effect of Belgian Poor Laws upon the character and condition of the people Sir Henry Barron quotes the following remarkable passage from the preamble of a bill introduced into the chamber by Baron Keroyne, late Minister of the Interior : 'Aussi a-t-on constate dans tous

---

* From Reports communicated to the Local Government Board by her Majesty's Secretary of State for Foreign Affairs ; with introductory remarks by Andrew Doyle, Esq., Local Government Inspector.

les pays, et notamment en Angleterre, ou l'intervention de la bienfaisance publique été poussée aux plus extremes exagérations que plus la charge est accablante pour la production et le travail plus elle reste stérile pour ceux qui en profitent; car l'indigent loin de ce relever par le secours public dans l'ordre moral, loin d'atteindre une situation meilleure à mesure que ce secours s'accroit et se perpétue, se sent entrainé disvantage par l'oisiveté dans la misère et dans la dègradation. Une longue expérience atteste égalemente en Belgique que les charges des communes ont subi une progression effrayante et que les sacrifices exigés des éléments les plus honnêtes de la population ont été trop souvent absorbés sans fruit par les individualités honteuses et méprisable.' "

A work by Mr. Fano, who is spoken of as " one of the highest authorities on matters relating to the condition of the poorer classes in Italy," is quoted as follows :

This writer describing the squalor and destitution of a large proportion of the peasantry and artisan population of Italy, says :—

" But we ought to make war implacably upon idleness and ignorance, because with us, as in all other nations, they are the first and chief causes of misery. The growth of that misery in our country is in a great measure due to those very institutions which were created for its suppression—the magnificent palaces which rise up on all sides in our cities to give refuge to suffering humanity. 'The life and soul of Italy,' said Moreau Christophe, ' are in her charitable institutions.' And, indeed, there is no kind of wretchedness or pain for which our fathers have not shown pity ; . . . . and this spirit of charity has been preserved, and displays itself more vividly every day. Still better than in institutions, it dwells in the hearts of all men. The result is that the property devoted to the relief of the poor amounts in every town in Italy to enormous sums which are swallowed up without profit, even if they do not produce injury and shame.

" But the crowd of beggars seems to multiply in proportion to the increase of the charities destined for the alleviation of their wants. . . . . The very profusion of charities is then one of the principal causes of the spread of mendicity in our country. When all feel sure that, in whatever disaster, they will find succor, and that they will obtain their sustenance from charity, if they do not earn it by their labor, there ceases to be any reason for being provident, and instead of relying upon his own strength every one accustoms himself to reckon upon the support of others. Thus are annihilated the vigor and the spirit of enterprise which are necessary for a man destined to lead a laborious life, and all sense of responsibility is lost. A man may beget children without taking the trouble to reflect whether he can feed them, because an Asylum and a maintenance will be found for them in the foundling hospital or in other institutions for the care of children. The prospect of sickness does not make him redouble his exertions and think of the necessity of saving and providing for an evil day because it appears to him sufficiently provided for by the hospital or the alms-house. . . . . But in order to obtain relief it is necessary to be poor, or at least to seem so, and the man who works has not the aspect of poverty. The workshop is then abandoned and the rags of common wretchedness are then put on ; and thus many persons voluntarily adopt a mendicant life, and finding it easier and more profitable than one of toil, choosing begging for their industry, and making it their estate. Their example is contagious; it is readily followed, for nothing renders a man more reluctant to work than the sight of indigence relieved. And thus misery increases in proportion to the relief which it finds, and misery and relief are alternately cause and effect.

"In Italy there are 1,355,341 indigent persons, but no system of legal charity exists. But the multitude of charitable institutions, their mode of administration, their great wealth, and the improvident manner in which their funds are frequently applied, are vices which have for us the same effects as those of legal charity, if not worse.

"If some of the riches which are squandered in such manner were directed to the purposes of education and the promotion of labor, they would be of more benefit to the classes which are now parasite, and would then become productive and moral. For I persist in thinking that in Italy mendicity is an imposture, and not produced by real destitution. And in support of this opinion might be adduced the fact that when Napoleon abolished the religious orders and the convent alms at Rome, out of 30,000 beggars left thus without assistance only 15,000 had themselves registered and taken into St. Joseph's Laterans. The same thing happened in Lombardy in the time of Joseph II. When the workhouses of Pizzighettone, Abbiategrasso and Milan were opened for beggars the greater part of them disappeared."

The following extracts from a standard work by E. Emminghaus,* are also very suggestive :

---

* Notes from " Poor Relief in Different Parts of Europe."

" In Basle, the richest town in Switzerland, we find proportionally the greatest number of persons relieved. In the flourishing Canton of Zurich, the proportion of persons relieved is least favorable in the three rich districts of Zurich, Horgen and Meilen, because as we learn from the Government Council Report of 1861, ' in these districts which hold the first place as regards prosperity, there is a much greater amount of relief given to the poor generally than is the case in many other districts.' The Zurich Government Council Report of 1865, mentions as directly conspicuous amongst the causes of poverty alleged by individual poor relieving bodies, ' the property belonging to corporations in individual communes, on which many a young man depends instead of seeking his fortune elsewhere.'

" In Canton Berne, too, it was found, after an inquiry was made in 1840, that there were ' the greatest number of persons relieved in proportion to the size of the civic unions : 1. In the town communes where rich endowments for the poor encourage them in habits of carelessness. 2. In communes, which in proportion to the size of the communal district have an unusually large number of freemen. 3. In communes which grant tolerably wide civic privileges. 4. In communes which on account of their remoteness afford but few sources of employment.' Still later, a pamphlet by the Bernese statesman, Blasch, mentions as ' a fact that wherever the greatest communal advantages exist, there the greatest indolence and dislike to work are to be found.'

" The excellent report of State Councilor Schaller on pauperism in Canton Fribourg, also calls attention to the fact ' that the number of poor is far greater in rich communes, such as Fribourg, Greyerz, Macon, &c., and

keeps up, though the means which the authorities there
have at their disposal ought to enable them by precau-
tionary measures, to strike at the very existence of pauperism."

Happily for the United States, the practice of
distributing Public Out-door Relief has not as yet
obtained a very firm hold among us, but it has
been the custom in many of our Cities to a limited
extent, and we can give some testimony which
shows that its evil effects are the same here as elsewhere.

In a paper read by Seth Low, Esq. of Brooklyn,
at the Conference of Charities and Correction in
1881, he says :

" Perhaps the most thorough inquiry which has been
made on American soil as to the operation of out-door
relief in this country, was instituted by the Secretary of
the Massachusetts State Board of Charities, in 1871, as to
the operation of the system in Massachusetts. Referring
to the condemnation of the system in England by such
writers as Professor Fawcett, by May, the author of the
" Constitutional History of England," and by Sir George
Nichols, the author of the " History of the English Poor
Law," the Secretary proposed a series of seven questions,
with the view of obtaining the results of the system of
out-door relief from the experience of the overseers of the
poor. Answers were received from one hundred and
sixty towns, enough to give a complete view of the system. An examination of the replies, as quoted in the
report, shows that the same evils in connection with out-
door relief recognized in England were largely recognized

in Massachusetts, but the weight of opinion was to the
effect that these evils in Massachusetts could still be kept
within bounds, while to do away altogether with out-door
relief was certain to result in great hardship to many deserving poor."

To this, we will add the testimony of George E.
McGonegal, the wisest and most experienced Su-
perintendent of the Poor of New York State.
Mr. McGonegal says :

* "We have a system in our State of furnishing what is
called temporary or out-door relief, the object of which is to
relieve families, who from sickness or other disability, become temporarily incapacitated from wholly maintaining
themselves. This is a worthy object, and deserving of all
praise ; but the great bulk of what is called temporary
relief, is not temporary, but permanent relief. Families
are furnished a stated amount weekly or monthly, and this
is continued week after week and year after year ; and I
know of nothing which does so much to encourage pauperism and educate paupers for the next generation, as
this system, which I think is in operation in most of the
counties, cities and towns in this State. There is nothing
except intemperance in the use of alcoholic liquors which
is more demoralizing to the head of a family, or more
ruinous to children, than to become imbued with the idea
that the public is bound to provide for them. And if
people could only realize, when they recommend, bring
or send a family, composed, in part, of bright, intelligent
children, who have never yet received public aid, to the

---

*From the proceedings of the Convention of the Superintendents of the
Poor of the State of New York, held at Rochester, N. Y., June 6, 7, 8,
1882. From paper read by Mr. McGonegal of Monroe county.

superintendent or overseer of the poor, and insist upon aid being furnished, that such an act was almost sure to ruin those bright children, and educate them for paupers or criminals when they become men and women, it seems to me that such people should exhaust every other resource to provide a way for such family to overcome its immediate difficulty, before incurring the fearful responsibility of being instrumental in making them paupers.

" People, very soon after commencing to receive public aid, lose their energy and self-respect, find it easier to rely upon the industry of others to furnish them their daily bread than to exert themselves to earn a livelihood ; their children learn to think that getting provisions and fuel from the overseer of the poor is perfectly right and proper, and they are almost certain to follow in the footsteps of their parents, especially as it requires a great deal less exertion than to earn their living by honest labor.

" There are cases where temporary relief is undoubtedly necessary, and if judiciously disbursed and discontinued at the earliest possible moment, before it becomes permanent relief and before the recipients become chronic paupers, then I have no doubt it is a real benefit to those who receive it. But after an experience of nearly twelve years in the care of the poor, and carefully studying, during that time, the effects of this so-called temporary relief, I am thoroughly convinced that the harm done by means of it greatly over-balances the good, and I think it is a question well worth considering, whether it would not be better to abolish it entirely. I believe that three-fourths of what is called temporary or out-door relief, furnished in the State of New York, is not only a direct injury to those who receive it, but is a great damage to society by encouraging indolence, and is an enormous unnecessary burden upon the industrious, provident class which is compelled to pay the expense."

A few words from the last annual report of the State Board of Charities and Reform of the State of Wisconsin are also suggestive :

"All experience shows that the demand for poor relief grows with the supply, and that a large amount for poor relief does not indicate a large amount of suffering which needs to be relieved, but a large amount of laxity or corruption on the part of officers and a large amount of willingness by able-bodied idlers to be fed at the public expense."

CHAPTER IV.

Public Out-door Relief.

CONCLUSIONS.

The argument which always has the most weight in favor of continuing. public out-door relief is that many deserving poor persons may suffer should it be cut off. It has already been proved by experience, however, that not only many suffer, but all suffer, by the continuance of a system which undermines the character of those it pretends to relieve, and at the same time drags down to their level many who never, but for its false allurements, would have been sufferers at all, while, on the contrary, the suffering which is looked for in consequence of the stopping of out-door relief does not occur. These seem to be anomalies, but they may be easily explained. The first fact, that poverty and suffering are increased and even caused by the relief intended to cure them, has already been shown to be due to the moral effects of such relief, and one of these effects is very clearly defined by Dr. Thomas Chalmers, the great Scotch divine, in his testimony before a Parliamentary Committee on the Poor Law for Ireland, as follows :

" I think it is one evil of public charity that the poor, who are not very accurate arithmeticians, are apt to overrate the power of a public charity, so that the real relaxation of their habits, not being proportional to the amount given, but being proportional to the amount expected, leaves them in greater misery than if no such public charity were instituted."

Another explanation of the evils of public relief is given in the following pregnant sentence of the report of the English Commissioners from which Mr. Low quoted, which contains, also, an indication of the direction from which real relief should come.

" The bane of all pauper legislation has been the legislating for extreme cases. Every exception, every violation of the general rule, to meet a real case of unusual hardship, lets in a whole class of fraudulent cases by which that rule must in time be destroyed. Where cases of real hardship occur, the remedy must be applied by individual charity, a virtue for which no system of compulsory relief can be or ought to be a substitute."

Here, as has been said, we have the solution of the difficulty. Private charity can and will provide for every case that should be kept from resorting to public sources of relief.

The statement that it can and will do this, is not based on the theory that it ought to, but on experience in the cities and towns in this country where public out-door relief has been abolished, not only without causing the suffering among special and worthy cases, which it is always feared will follow such a radical change, but with the most beneficial effects on the character, and as a natural consequence, on the condition of the people who formerly depended on it.

In Kings county, in our own State, containing a city of almost half a million inhabitants, we have one example; in Philadelphia, with her 890,000 inhabitants, another; and in smaller communities the same effects follow the same causes.

We have comparatively full statistics from Kings county of the amount expended each year for her dependent classes, both from public ·and private funds in and out of institutions, for the ten years ending September 30, 1882. Until 1879, public out-door relief was given by the county to the amount of $100,000 or more yearly; it was then cut off in the middle of winter, without warning, without any substitute being provided, and the result was—nothing.

In fact, except for the saving of the money and the stopping of petty political corruption which had been carried on by means of the relief, and the cessation of the spectacle of hundreds of people passing through the streets with baskets of provisions furnished by the public, it would have been impossible to discover that the relief had been stopped, And there was, besides, in 1879 and 1880, a smaller number of persons supported in the alms-house than in any other of the ten years from 1873 to 1882.

The following table, showing approximately the amounts spent by the County and from private sources during that period in charity, will repay a careful study:

KINGS COUNTY.	Census 1870.		Census.		
	396,099		482,493		
EXPENSES FOR.	1873.	1874.	1875.	1876.	1877.
County alms-house..........	$304,588 00	$290,950 00	$295,636 00	$268,655 00	$280,097 00
County out-door relief........	100,555 00	134,935 00	116,524 00	98,815 00	141,137 00
Private institutions........ ...	412,274 00	395,570 00	529,590 00	515,105 00	523,374 00
Private out-door relief societies	54,615 00	53,800 00	49,353 00	44,545 00	43,203 00
	$872,032 00	$875,255 00	$991,103 00	$927,120 00	$987,811 00

KINGS COUNTY.			Census.		
			566,689		
EXPENSES FOR.	1878.	1879.	1880.	1881.	1882.
County almshouse	$255,470 00	$245,843 00	$207,900 00	$265,997 00	$287,236 co
County out-door relief......	57,054 00	.. ..	....	....	....
Private institutions........	524,400 00	493,440 00	613,320 00	558,507 00	1,007,609 00
Private out-door relief societies	44,295 00	47,779 00	41,171 00	46,367 00	45,695 00
	$881,219 00	$787,062 00	$862,391 00	$870,871 00	*$1,340,540 00

It shows that, with an increase of population of about one hundred thousand, the amount of relief

*NOTE.—Increase of expense in 1832 due to the building of a large hospital by a private individual, at a cost of several hundred thousand dollars.

given in 1880, in Kings county, was not so large as in 1873, and that the largest amounts spent were in 1875, 1877 and 1882.

There could scarcely be a stronger proof that the stopping of out-door relief does not cause the suffering that is anticipated, or, in other words, that the need supplied by public out-door relief is in fact created by it.

The following letter from the Secretary of the Philadelphia Society for Organizing Charity, gives the results of the abolition of public out-door relief in that city :

CENTRAL OFFICE, NO 1602 CHESTNUT ST.,
PHILADELPHIA, 23*d October*, 1883.

MRS. J. S. LOWELL, *Commissioner, etc.*, 120 *E. 30th St., New York, N. Y.:*

DEAR MADAM—In reply to your favor of the 19th inst., I can say that the out-door poor-law relief in this city amounted to from fifty to eighty thousand dollars annually for many years preceding 1880, when it was discontinued.   It was dispensed by twelve officials, termed "visitors," appointed, in most instances, for *political* reasons.   At the time it was abolished, we, for a few weeks, felt an increased pressure for relief upon the private charities; but that was only temporary, and although the population of the city has increased during the past three years, the numbers of the in-door poor have decreased.

Very respectfully yours,

JAS. W. WALK, M. D.,
General Secretary.

Here we have the experiences of two of the largest cities in the United States, and it may be well to add to this record that of New York City, in which the public out-door relief for some years has not exceeded $65,000 yearly, and has been confined to the distribution of coal, of medical relief, and of a small annual cash donation to certain blind persons, all of which, in the opinion of many well-informed persons, it would be well to discontinue, trusting to private charity to supply whatever might be required in its place.

We have shown above that public out-door relief may, with advantage, be discontinued in large cities—and we have also the record of two smaller and rural or mixed communities, which point to the same conclusion.

The town of Castleton, in Richmond county, N. Y., has a population of 12,679, and, since 1879, not one cent of public out-door relief has been given in the town. In former years, the public relief varied from $1,500 to $3,000 per annum, with from one hundred to three hundred persons on the pauper list.

The poor have not suffered by the entire cessation of public relief; but there is less idleness, and the proportion of the poor from Castleton who are in the poorhouse is smaller than that from the other towns of the county, where public out-door relief is still distributed.

In Herkimer county, N. Y., there was in 1870 a population of 39,929, and public out-door relief amounted to $21,290; in 1875, the population was 41,589, and the relief $1,084; in 1882 the population was 42,667, and the relief $2,000.

The following letter from the Superintendent of the Poor requires no explanation:

OFFICE OF THE SUPERINTENDENT OF THE POOR, }
HERKIMER, N. Y., *October* 25, 1883.   }

Mrs. C. R. LOWELL, *Commissioner, etc., New York City:*

Your favor of the 23d inst. at hand, and in reply would say that I have compared the figures quoted by you with the itemized accounts published in the proceedings of the Board of Supervisors, and find them substantially correct.

"As to the cause of the change," or the difference in the amount expended in 1870 and 1882, it may be a little difficult to make an explanation that would be entirely just and satisfactory to all concerned. In the year 1870, very loose and extravagant notions of expenditures in all departments of government prevailed, and our county was no exception; double the numbers of people were kept in the county poor-house, and the cost of supplies being no greater than now, it cost nearly double the amount *per capita* to keep them that it does now. In the year 1878, when all kinds of supplies reached the lowest point, it cost $2 per week in our poor-house; in 1882, it cost $1.27½ per week, and they were kept in a building warmed by steam and lighted by gas. The following facts may explain the situation to some extent, viz.:

   1. The building of a new county poorhouse.

2. Sending all disabled transients to the poor house instead of keeping them in hotels or boarding-houses.

3. Cutting off all those able to work and making them earn their living or go to the poor-house.

4. No men supported because they vote this or that ticket.

5. When a family apply for relief, their circumstances are fully investigated and a record kept, so that we know the exact condition of all such families.

6. We grant outside relief only to those having a family of young children; in such cases we consider it more economical and humane to keep the family together if the circumstances will warrant it.

The above facts may have something to do with producing the results which you note.

As to the effects of cutting off such large expenditures, I can safely say that there are not as many paupers in our poorhouse, that there are not as many destitute in our villages, and that there are no complaints from any class of people.

There is but one drawback to our present condition, and that is that the number of our insane is increasing; while pauperism is slightly decreasing, insanity is increasing with us.

Very respectfully yours,

JOHN CROWLEY,

Superintendent.

Out-door relief, then, it appears from the foregoing facts and arguments, fails to attain any one of the objects which should be aimed at by relief from the public funds.

1. It fails to provide that no one shall starve or suffer for the common necessaries of life, because, however lavish may be the relief, unless self-restraint and providence be conferred upon those who receive it, all that is bestowed will often be wasted by them in riotous living, and the innocent and helpless beings dependent upon them be left to suffer far more than had the relief been denied.

2. It fails to save the recipient of relief and the community from moral harm, because human nature is so constituted that no man can receive as a gift what he should earn by his own labor without a moral deterioration, and the presence in the community of certain persons living on public relief, has the tendency. to tempt others to sink to their degraded level.

3. Out-door relief can not be of short duration, because when it has once been accepted, the barrier is broken down, and rarely, or never, thereafter, is the effort made to do without it, and thus all such relief has the tendency to become regular and permanent.

4. The tax payers are the losers by out-door relief, because, although the amount given to each individual is, undoubtedly, smaller than would be required for that individual in an institution, yet out-door relief is so infectious, and, once obtained is so easy a way of getting a living, that far larger numbers demand and receive it than could be in-

duced to enter an institution, and thus the total cost of public relief is always increased by giving it outside of the workhouse or almshouse.

5. The chief object, to convince the public that the poor are adequately cared for by public officials, has never been attained by either system, and may be left for time, experience and education.

Out-door relief, in fact, can not be defended ; it has none of the redeeming features of private charity, because there is nothing personal or softening in it, nor has it the advantages which might, perhaps, be derived from an acknowledged and openly advocated communism, for the principle underlying it is not that the proceeds of all men's labor is to be fairly divided among all, but that the idle, improvident and even vicious man has the right to live in idleness and vice upon the proceeds of the labor of his industrious and virtuous fellow-citizen.

We have, already, accepted in this paper the postulate that the community should save every one of its members from starvation, no matter how low or depraved such member may be, but we contend that the necessary relief should be surrounded by circumstances that shall not only repel every one, not in extremity, from accepting it, but which shall also insure a distinct moral and physical improvement on the part of all those who are forced to have recourse to it—that is, discipline and education should be inseparably associated with any system of public relief.

And there is still another point to be insisted on ; while the acknowledgment is made that every person born into a civilized community has a right to live, yet the community has the right to say that incompetent and dangerous persons shall not, so far as can be helped, be born to acquire this right to live upon others. To prevent a constant and alarming increase of these two classes of persons, the only way is for the community to refuse to support any except those whom it can control— that is, except those who will submit themselves to discipline and education. It is certainly an anomaly, for a man and woman who have proved themselves incapable of supplying their own daily needs, to bring into the world other helpless beings, to be also maintained by a tax upon the community.

If, then, out-door relief is proved to be not only useless, as a means of relieving actual, existing suffering, but an active means of increasing present and future want and vice, the only other means of giving public relief is within an institution, and this will be found to render possible the attainment of all the objects which should be aimed at by public relief.

It is easy to provide that all the inmates shall have the necessaries of life, and besides being fed

and clothed, they can be subjected to the best sanitary regulations, they can be kept clean and be
required to live regularly, to work, to exercise, to
sleep, as much or as little as is good for them, and
this brings us to the second object, for in an institution the inmates besides being prevented from
receiving moral harm, can be brought under such
physical, moral, mental and industrial training as
will render them far better members of society
than they ever were before, and will eventually
make them self-supporting, and so attain the third
object.

The fourth object (saving money to the workers
of the community) will, of course, follow from the
measures enumerated above. To cure paupers
and make them self-supporting, however costly
the process, must always be economical as compared with a smaller but constantly increasing and
continual outlay for their maintenance.

CHAPTER V.

Public Relief.

PRINCIPLES.

To accomplish the objects set forth in the last chapter as desirable, it is not sufficient simply to shelter, feed and clothe the public dependents inside of institutions supported by taxation. Such institutions may, and unhappily do, often, become the means of still further degrading the miserable beings who crowd into them.

To make them useful at all, it is necessary that they should be governed by those who recognize that the prevention and permanent cure of pauperism, vice and disease are the objects to be sought, and the whole system of public relief must be based upon that principle.

In every city or county there should be three Departments, to be named respectively:

The Department for the Care of Children;

The Department for the Care of Public Dependents;

The Department for the Reduction of Crime.

These Departments should each be governed by a separate Board, the members to be men and women, appointed by the Mayor of the city and to be removed only for incompetence or for violation or neglect of duty, and required to give their whole time to their office, receiving a sufficient salary to justify this demand.

I. With the Department for the Care of Children would rest the duty of so dealing with the little ones entrusted to it, that they may gradually but surely be cut off from the influences which have brought their parents to a condition of dependence, and be absorbed into the bulk of the population, with no memory even, if it can be avoided, of any thing suggestive of pauperism or crime. No child should ever for a moment be allowed to associate with paupers and criminals, and the States of New York and Massachusetts and Pennsylvania have been wise in forbidding the sending of children to poorhouses and jails for destitution and vagrancy. They should go further, however, and provide that no official who has charge of paupers or criminals should have authority of any sort over a dependent child. The creation of a separate department for their care I believe to be a necessity, but not for the purpose of housing them in public institutions; this department should have but one institution (apart from schools, to be spoken of further on) under its control—a central temporary home, into which should be received all children who have any claim upon public support, pending the examination of that claim. From this temporary home, those found to be really destitute should be quickly transferred to suitable private institutions and until some other disposition could be made of them, the public should pay for their support in such institutions.

In a measure this is the present practice in New York City and in many other cities of New York State, but there is nowhere, so far as I know, a separate department created to have the care of these children, and most unfortunately, in New York City at least, the custom has grown up of requiring that judges shall commit children to private institutions, as a necessary condition of obtaining payment from the city for their support. This undoubtedly is a dangerous proceeding, since the familiarization with a court of law tends to destroy the dread of arrest, which should be fostered as one of the strongest deterrent influences against crime. To bring a child before a judge in a criminal court in order to secure his entrance into an institution of charity is a most unwise measure.

How to care for the children of the very poor, and often depraved, part of the population of cities, is one of the most serious of public questions; and, in discussing it, it is necessary to consider the effect to be produced not only upon the child, but upon its parents and upon the public at large.

The first and instinctive impulse is to collect all children who are subject even to occasional sufferings, neglect, or evil example, and to surround them with bright and good influences, guarding them from danger and trial through their tender youth. This seems to many to be the duty of the community both to itself and to the children of misfortune, but is it so in reality? Is the child itself to be saved by thus removing it from its natural surroundings? Such removals often unfit it for the battle of life. Again, shall we relieve the parent of the responsibility which God has imposed upon him? In seeking to save the child by this means, the parent is too often sacrificed and deprived of the strongest incentive he can possibly have to exertion and right living.

The effect upon the tax-payer and upon the hard working poor man, struggling to bring up his children to be honest, industrious and healthy, must not be ignored. The tax-payer should not be required to give what he needs for his own family to support the family of his dissolute neighbor, unless that family threatens to be a public injury; nor should the honest laborer see the children of the drunkard enjoying advantages which his own may not hope for. There can never be any hard and fast lines laid down in regard to this question, for while, on the one hand, children must be protected from cruelty and from evil training, on the other, a constant watch must be kept that parents who are capable of rightly bringing up their children are not tempted to give up that duty because it is a hard one, and it is to be remembered that the poorest home, unless it be a degraded one, is better than the best institution.

There can be no question that public institutions and institutions maintained by the public money, should not be sectarian in character, and that all children dependent upon the public funds for support should be required to attend the public schools. There should moreover be a constant pressure brought to bear on parents to contribute toward the support of their children, and as soon as they are able, they should be required to take them back, or if unable or unfit to do this after a given number of years, they should forfeit all claim to them. No child should be held as a public charge for an indefinite time, and the parent have the right to reclaim it at any moment. A parent who will not perform the duties of a parent should not have the rights of a parent. All this field of labor should belong to the Department for the Care of Children, which should periodically examine into the circumstances of all parents whose children are a public charge, decide whether payment should be exacted or not, whether the child should return to its home or be entirely removed from its parents, find permanent places for all children who remain a charge upon the public after three years, and watch over them in their new homes. This department should also be required to draw up rules and by-laws for all institutions receiving children to board at public expense, and see that they are carried out to the letter.

Besides these duties in regard to children who are fit subjects for public support, the Department for the Care of Children should have the control and management of Industrial Day Schools for the children of persons who, though able to support them, neglect, or do not know how, to train them to be useful, industrious, and honest. These schools should be especially designed to supply the wants of their home training, and attendance should be made compulsory on all vagrant and truant children. By such means, the Department for the Care of Children would be a potent factor in the work of diminishing crime and pauperism.

II. The Department for the Care of Public Dependents should have charge of the public hospital, insane asylum, almshouse and workhouse, the last to receive only persons committed as destitute. There are two means of reducing pauperism: 1st, by preventing accessions to the ranks of paupers from without, which can be accomplished by rendering pauperism unattractive and by the general enlightenment of the people, and 2nd, by restoring individual paupers to manhood and

independence. The aim being to *cure* the individual, whether of sickness, insanity, intemperance,
or simply of the tendency to be shiftless and lazy,
the same system should be enforced in all the various buildings under the charge of the department ;
strict discipline should be enforced, absolute cleanliness demanded, industry be inculcated, not for
the purpose of saving money, but to teach the
individual. To train the mental and moral nature
should be the first object, and no other should be
allowed to take precedence of it.

Thus, in the hospitals, the classification of cases
should not be made with regard to the convenience
of the physicians, but with a view to preventing
contamination. Men and women who have become
ill by intemperance or vice should not be treated
as ordinary patients, or allowed to associate with
the latter. The convalescents, especially the
young, should be taught and employed so far as
possible.

In the insane asylums, teaching, moral instruction and employment would usually be found the
most efficacious means for the cure of disease, and
thus even here the attempt to raise the individual
and mould his character would result in the diminution of the expense of supporting the asylum.

I do not think that we sufficiently recognize the
fact that, in public asylums at any rate, insanity in
the majority of cases is due to excessive indulgence

in one form or other of vice, and that frequently the insane are persons who have so long neglected self-control that they finally lose all power of self-control. I am sure, however, that this is so, and I believe that there is as much room for reformatory treatment in an insane asylum as in any other institution.

The fact that a large part of the population of all public institutions are driven to them through their own folly and sin, renders it an imperative duty to seek to elevate these unfortunates so far as possible, and, still more, to prevent their contaminating others less degraded than themselves. Whatever may be the temptations that beset the weak and wicked outside the walls of an institution not one evil influence should be allowed to approach those who are under the charge of a great city. A wrong that is done by the authority of law is an outrage against humanity, and no wrong is so black as one that hurts the soul.

III. The Department for the Reduction of Crime would have, as its name imports, a wide field of labor—to my mind it would be the most important of the three departments which I propose—and I have chosen this name for it, in order that every one, inside of it and outside of it, may fully recognize what is the main end of its creation, and that the care of criminals and the supervision of prisons may be put in their proper subordinate places, as one means only of accomplishing the real work of the department. I would place under the charge of this branch of the government not only the reformatory institutions in the city or county (including those for juvenile offenders), but the station-houses and the police force, which latter should be its agents to prevent, as well as to detect crime, to protect the weak who cannot resist temptation unaided, to watch habitual criminals when at large, and to guard those undergoing sentence. This department should also have the entire control of licensing the liquor business, that most potent of the causes of crime.

If it were possible, it would be well that the judges should in some way be connected with this department, and, in any event, the management of the courts should be a part of its business.   The harm done by our courts, as at present governed, is not at all recognized.   The publicity to which all persons on trial are exposed is in itself a serious evil, especially in the case of children and young women, breaking down and destroying all natural modesty and making them in very deed "brazen faced," while it also fosters the love of notoriety which is so common in weak natures as to be acknowledged as a very strong incentive to crime among a certain class.

The trials of women and children, at least, should be conducted in comparative privacy—only certain persons being allowed to be present. We have passed the time when we need a public trial to insure justice for the accused.

There is no doubt also that the station-houses are, in many cities, places of contamination and degradation. There should be special buildings for the temporary imprisonment of women, and women-officers should be employed to guard them ; and here, as well as in conveying prisoners to and from the Reformatories, they should be protected from contamination by every known means. I speak only of Reformatories, for there should be no prison which is not a reformatory. All sentences, also, should be for an indeterminate period, leaving the authorities power to place the prisoners out on probation, and to discharge them finally.

If the object be, as it should be, to protect society, why should not an irresponsible criminal be treated as an irresponsible insane patient is dealt with? the superintendent in charge of each deciding when he may safely be trusted at large. With proper regulations and efficient supervision by the police to save them from their own weakness, undoubtedly a large number of criminals who are now shut up, in demoralizing idleness and vile companionship, might be safely allowed at liberty ; thus saving them from debasing influences, and the State from the necessity of supporting them. But there is a smaller number, who now are periodically turned loose to prey upon their fellows, who are as dangerous as any madman, and who ought to be always kept under control. Thus our folly is apparent in both directions—we keep masses of men shut up under a system which destroys both soul and body, who are quite capable of being useful and valuable members of society, while we constantly unchain wild beasts, knowing them to be such, waiting for some overt act before we dare to lay our hands upon them again.

Under the rule of the Department for the Reduction of Crime, the number of criminals imprisoned would surely be greatly diminished, and the training of all actually in restraint would be such as to teach them the lessons they failed to learn from the influences of a natural life ; while those who could not learn would never be allowed the opportunity to injure themselves and their fellow-men. Our present system of treating prisoners is generally the exact opposite of this and of the practice in Gloucestershire, England, where crime has diminished most remarkably during the past forty years. Mr. T. B. Ll. Baker, the man who has been mainly instrumental in bringing about the great change, thus describes the means adopted, in a paper written in 1878 :

"In 1783, Sir George Paul, one of the Justices of this county, brought before the Grand Jury his scheme for bringing Howard's suggestions into practice; and in 1785

he obtained an Act of Parliament for building a new gaol
on what was then called the Solitary System. . . .
In 1843 it became necessary to enlarge our accommoda-
tion. . . . We were urged to pull down all our old
prisons and to build one large prison, at a cost of about
£140,000; while it was estimated that the number of com-
mitments would be doubled in about every sixteen years.
We did not do this, but we added largely to all our five
prisons, and at an expense of £40,585 we raised the number of cells to 720. . . . We were told we had not
built enough, and we should, in ten years' time, be required to add to it. But, instead of this, our police was
organized, and preventive measures adopted—raising, indeed, at first, the number committed, but reducing them
after a few years. By 1861 we were enabled to close four
of our five gaols, and our average number in prison for
the last ten years has been under 200 for a population of
352,000. . . . Our number in prison has diminished,
notwithstanding the increase of population, from between
500 and 600 in 1840, to 166 in 1876, and I have no doubt
that a considerable portion of this decrease may be at-
tributed to the fact that, until 1846, we were not allowed
to keep the accused in individual confinement by day,
though by night they were always separated. The men,
indeed, were divided into two day rooms, presumed to be
for greater or lesser crimes, and the boys were kept in a
third room; but what was even then spoken of as 'the in-
conceivable abomination of the habit of indiscriminate
association,' especially among the boys, was very sad.
Still, so many other good influences commenced work at
nearly the same time, viz: the establishment of a police
(endeavoring still more to prevent than to detect crime),
of reformatories for juveniles, . . . and more lately

the adoption of cumulative punishment for the heavier class of crimes (we have not yet obtained the power of thus dealing with the minor offenses), and all have no doubt contributed so much to the result, that we can not assign the share of each. . . .

" I hold strongly that our great object is not that of having the most perfectly planned and ordered goals ; our object is the reduction of crime to the greatest degree that we can effect. Goals and prisons are *one* means to that end, but *only one means*, and so far as my experience goes, not the most efficacious, nor the least objectionable. Our means to reduce crime are :

1st. A well-arranged system of sentences.

2d. A trustworthy and reasoning police, and

3dly. The goal."

In a letter dated April, 1880, Mr. Baker, writing to an American, says :

" I feel quite certain that, with the same amount of crime we now have, we might have less than half of our present proportion in prison, and that the lessening of our regular average in prison would lessen our crime. But I cannot believe that in America generally you have nearly the amount of crime that we have ; and if so, far less than half the average in prison ought to suffice for you. Certainly the common prisons are a terrible evil, but I can not believe that the country which gave, not only so much money, but so many noble lives, to the cause of extirpating slavery, can continue much longer not only to imprison the bodies, but also to ruin the souls of its own citizens, when a great improvement might, as I believe, be made with very slight expenditure in the first place, and with actually considerable saving in the end. Perhaps I am more cheered in this belief at the present moment by a letter that I yesterday received from the Governor of the prison at Gloucester. Our average number in prison in 1870 was 279; in 1875 it was 209. Since then it has gradually lowered to 170, 160, etc., but for the last three months the average of prisoners belonging to our county has been 131, and yesterday it was just 100—a smaller number than, I think, it has been during the present century. Of course we must not consider this a permanent lowering, but only a pleasant omen."

PART II.

PRIVATE CHARITY.

CHAPTER I.

INSTITUTIONS.

It is very desirable that the official and volunteer efforts to lift up the degraded part of the population of any town or city should supplement each other and mutually supply the deficiencies inherent in each.

The public institutions should always be under the constant oversight of volunteer visitors, who should not only represent the people at large and seek to discover and make public all wanton abuses and official neglect and carelessness, but who should also supply the precious element of human sympathy and tender personal interest which must often be lacking where the care of dependence is a business and the common everyday work the means of livelihood of overtaxed officials. The more entirely, however, these volunteer visitors will receive these same officers within the pale of human sympathy, and the more frequently they will accord a thought to their troubles and difficulties, the more sure will they be of benefiting also the dependent patients and inmates of the institutions they visit. It is a great mistake on the part of those who wish to accomplish any good to assume an attitude of antagonism toward the officials in public institutions—a mistake in policy and in fact, for the amount of unselfishness and devotion often to be found among those who spend their lives in the distasteful ministry to ungrateful and degraded pauper insane and sick, can scarcely be imagined.

On the other hand, private charitable institutions need regular and severe official inspection. The tendency to slackness, extravagance, and even more serious abuses can scarcely be resisted, unless the standard is kept up by constant criticism from persons who know what they are talking about, and who have no interest in making matters appear better than they are. Those who undertake the care of dependents of any class, children, the sick, old people or insane, have assumed a quasi-public trust, and they must be helped to a conscientious discharge of it. It is not their own private affair whether those whom they have taken under their protection are well or ill cared for; it is a public concern and good care should be insured by public inspection.

This is still more the case when public funds are

placed in the hands of private individuals to spend for the care of dependents, and here, besides the inspection required in other institutions, a rigid financial supervision should be maintained.

As to the policy of granting public funds to private charities, it is scarcely a question that it is a grave error to supply the entire support of public dependents in private institutions, or to provide by law, as is done in New York, for a per capita allowance for each inmate admitted, sufficient for his support, for this must act as an encouragement to increase the number of inmates unduly, since a larger number can be proportionally more cheaply supported than a small number, and consequently a direct pecuniary gain follows upon the increased size of these institutions.

The correct rule would appear to be to furnish from the public funds to any established private institutions, a certain proportion (never more than half) of the cost of maintaining the inmates, provided that the official inspectors report favorably each year upon the condition of the institution and the inmates, and that some proper test as to the wisdom of admissions is devised, and a limit is placed upon the time during which the payments are to continue. The Government grants made to the certified schools of England seem to be guarded by proper restrictions.

There is, moreover, a serious moral objection to

private institutions supported entirely by public funds, because they hold out more of a temptation to the struggling poor than are offered by public institutions—many persons who would turn with horror from a poorhouse would willingly enter a "Home" —the disgrace of dependence is thought to be less in the latter case.   And while this may be so, if the " Home " is really supported by private charity, it is most certainly not so if the " Home " is in fact an almshouse, maintained by money raised by taxation, and it is desirable that its true character should not be cloaked.

CHAPTER II.

Before we can speak of Charity to the poor, we must find out what it is—that is, we must agree upon some definition of the word.

1st. It must be voluntary. No benefit conferred because it could not be avoided could be called charitable. Were the poor to take by force the possessions of the rich, although they might benefit by them, neither of the parties to the transaction would delude themselves with the idea that charity had been bestowed or received.

2nd. It must be free in another sense. The person to whom we exercise charity cannot have an acknowledged personal claim upon us. The fulfilling of the duties of parent or child would not be spoken of as " charity " whatever might be the suffering on the one hand and the devotion on the other, nor can a master be charitable to his servants or work-people, unless he does for them more than it is his duty to do. He can be kind, just, fair, and considerate, but not charitable unless they fall into distress and he voluntarily helps them out of it, and even then the distress must not have arisen for his sake or in his service—if a man were killed in the service of his employer and the latter were to undertake to provide for his family, the act would scarcely be called charitable —it would be merely discharging a debt.

3rd. Charity must go further than kind feeling —it must be kind action—it must accomplish good to the object of it. No amount of good feeling could convert an injurious act into a charitable one.

4th. Charity must be exercised toward a person in inferior circumstances to those of his benefactor. We cannot be charitable to our equals—in the sense of the word with which we are dealing.

Charity, then, as I define it, must be a voluntary, free, beneficent action performed toward those who are in more destitute circumstances and inferior in worldly position.

By this definition, of course, all official and public relief is put outside the pale of charity, since it lacks the voluntary element.

By this definition, moreover, I contend, that all indiscriminate almsgiving and all systematic dole-giving is proved not to be charitable.

Charity must be a good—a good forever, to him who receives it—but however benevolent may be the motive, if the action be not beneficent, there is no charity. Almsgiving and dolegiving are hurt-ful—therefore they are not charitable.

Almsgiving and dolegiving are hurtful even to those who do not receive them, because they help to keep down wages by enabling those who do receive them to work for less than fair pay. No greater wrong can be done, not only to those who receive the miserable pittance, but to all working people. Wages at the best are low enough, without being reduced by the action of the benevolent.

Almsgiving and dolegiving are hurtful to those who receive them because they lead men to remit their own exertions and depend on others, upon whom they have no real claim, for the necessaries of life, *which they do not receive after all.*

In this last fact lies one secret of the injury done—false hopes are excited, the unhappy recipients of alms become dependent, lose their energy, are rendered incapable of self-support, and what they receive in return for their lost character is quite inadequate to supply their needs; thus they are kept on the verge almost of death by the very persons who think they are relieving them, by the kindly souls who are benevolent, but who will not take the trouble to be beneficent, too.

The nature of doles is to be insufficient and to be uncertain. They would cease to be doles and would become pensions were they to assume a regular character and to be sufficient to meet the ascertained wants of the recipient, and in certain cases pensions are an excellent manner of bestow-

ing charity. Indeed, where it is possible for charitable societies to support entirely such people as
they decide to help, the effect on the latter individuals may not be any worse than if they had
fallen heir to an adequate income in any other
way, although it is of course a fact that sudden
inheritances often do destroy good habits both
among the rich and the poor ; but even under
these circumstances, the effect on others would
have to be considered. The extraordinary and
fearful result of assuring every family, however
improvident and however vicious, a comfortable
support, has been shown in the quotation from the
Report of the English Poor Law Commission,
given in Part First of this book. The terrifying
decay of industry, temperance, providence and
natural affection not only among what are technically called " the poor" in England during the fifty
years preceding 1835 but also among a large proportion of all the men and women who labored for
their daily bread, is a warning that must not be
overlooked.

The great point ,to be considered is what is
possible. Could all men be made comfortable and
happy by a charity so extended that it would
amount to an equal division of the wealth of any
given community, I should welcome the measure
with my whole heart ; but it has been proved, and
surely it scarcely needed proving, that no amount

of money scattered among people who are without character and virtue, will insure even physical comfort.

It is for this reason that nothing should be done under the guise of charity, which tends to break down character. It is the greatest wrong that can be done to him to undermine the character of a poor man—for it is his all. The struggle is hard, he needs all his determination and strength of will to fight his way, and nothing that deprives him of these qualities can be "charitable."

The proof that dolegiving and almsgiving do break down independence, do destroy energy, do undermine character, may be found in the growing ranks of pauperism in every city, in the fact that the larger the funds given in relief in any community, the more pressing is the demand for them, and in the experience and testimony of all practical workers among the poor.

Before entering on any explanation of how the poor may be raised and helped, we must form some idea of who the poor are. There is a mistaken and dangerous, but I fear not uncommon, impression, that in every community there exists a given and constant number of individuals who may be classed under that name, who are absolutely helpless, and whom it is *somebody's* duty to feed, clothe, and generally care for.

The line of division between this mass of suffering people and every body else is supposed to be clearly defined, and the former are to be treated on quite different principles from the rest of the world. Thus, while it is thought to be a good thing to drive a hard bargain with the widow who does the family washing, and to make her earn her dollar by a hard day's work, it is also thought to be a good thing to give a dollar without inquiry or equivalent to the widow who passes her days in idleness and her nights in debauchery. The fact that the first widow may in time come to contrast her lot with that of the second widow, and may prefer the latter, seldom occurs to the almsgiver, nor does he know how desperate a temptation he is presenting daily to his fellow men.

As a fact we have the miserable company of hopeless paupers that is imagined by the common mind, but it is most unfortunately not fixed in quantity ; it is perpetually being augmented by the weak and foolish and wicked who have watched the course of benevolent persons and societies, and who can no longer resist the temptation constantly held out to them to give up the unpleasant struggle and accept the gift so freely offered of a living without labor. Therefore the problem before those who would be charitable, is not how to deal with a given number of poor ; it is how to help those who are poor, without adding to their numbers and constantly increasing the evils they seek to cure.

Whatever the circumstances, whether in a sparsely settled neighborhood or in a crowded city, the principle adopted must be the same, although the action will have to be different.

The fundamental principle is that all charity must tend to raise the character and elevate the moral nature, and so improve the condition of those toward whom it is exercised, and must not tend to injure the character or condition of others.

Clinging to this principle as a guide, there are several rules which it is well to follow in practical work. I will mention some of the most important only.

The first is that each case is to be *radically* dealt with; that is, finding fellow beings in want and suffering, the cause of the want and suffering are to be removed if possible even if the process be as painful as plucking out an eye or cutting off a limb.

The cause of distress is to be sought out and dealt with, or the distressed ones to be let alone, for only harm will result from unwise and ignorant meddling. Better leave people to the hard working of natural laws than to run the risk of interfering with those laws in a mischievous manner. This first rule, that each case must be radically dealt with and finally disposed of, shows one fundamental difference in the mental attitude of those who believe and who disbelieve in "dolegiving." The former regard it as a natural condition of things that a certain part of the community should not be self-supporting, they think it even desirable that there should be "the poor" to look after, they accept the degradation and suffering of other people with calmness, as inevitable facts, and to satisfy their own feelings of pity they offer their inadequate doles, never casting a thought beyond the present day, or even inquiring whether permanent and efficient help might not be almost as easy to give.

The other class, on the other hand, regard each case of poverty as a wrong, an unnatural evil and one which they should use every effort to eradicate; it shocks them that men should be unable to live by their labor; but they do not give doles, knowing that this will often retard or entirely prevent the energetic action required on the part of the sufferers themselves to lift themselves out of their difficulties.

The dole-giving acts upon the receiver as insufficient watering in dry weather acts upon plants—they die because they are watered and are tempted to keep their roots near the surface, instead of plunging them deep down where they will find nourishment. With plants, you must either water thoroughly or not at all—with the human beings you must either care for them entirely or let them depend on themselves—to tempt them with a false hope that you will supply them with what they need, and then fail them, is cruelty.

The second rule is, that the best help of all is to help people to help themselves.   That is, that instead of receiving the means of living, men should receive from the benevolent the means of earning a living—that the poor man or woman should have the road cleared so that they may themselves march on to success—that their brains should be released from ignorance, their hands freed from the shackles of incompetence, their bodies saved from the pains of sickness, and their souls delivered from the bonds of sin.

CHAPTER III.

METHODS IN COUNTRY AND CITY.

To be charitable in any degree, the first necessity is knowledge of the facts, not only of those connected with a special case of suffering, but of the surroundings and antecedents, character and possibilities of the people to be helped. No wise course, no radical measures, no permanent help are possible without this.

In the country or even in a village this knowledge exists—it is not necessary to adopt any special means to acquire it. In fact this naturally obtained knowledge makes the whole problem of dealing with the one or two poor families so easy, that the danger (or certainty) is, that it will not be thought worth while to adopt the right principles, or indeed any principle. It seems most easy and natural and right in one's own neighborhood, where one knows every one, to step into the house of a poor friend and give him the help he requires in his unexpected distress, and it is natural and right, provided one does know every one; but gradually there come strangers, both rich and poor, to live in the village; suddenly the knowing everyone is discovered to have become a thing of the past, and the new rich neighbors upset the well considered plans that have been formed for the old poor neighbors, and the poor neighbors, hearing how much kindness there is in the town, ask also to share it, and suddenly the community awakes to the fact that they have a pauper class in their midst, and that some of their old inhabitants belong to it, and the painful suspicion forces itself upon the benevolent that they have perhaps helped to drive them into it.

The only way to undo the harm is to regain by some means the advantage that the small community had without effort. The same intimate knowledge of those who have to be helped must be got in some way, and the only possible means of getting this knowledge, and of making it available to others, is that recommended by Dr. Chalmers and carried out in Glasgow and in Elberfeld, that is, of subdividing the labor among many willing hands.

A small association of men and women should be formed and a special territory assigned to each, so that he may become thoroughly acquainted with all who live within its limits. It will be far better if such an association does not call itself a Relief Society or an Employment Society, or any sort of society that will tempt people to begin to consider their own needs and whether a little help would not be very convenient to them also. Such

Societies as these last are a standing advertisement for applicants, and the supply is always equal to the demand. Let this new association merely be a Friendly Society and let its objects be to work for the good of the whole town, to create a neighborly good feeling, to help forward all good objects and put down all bad ones, to see that the laws are enforced, sanitary regulations complied with, that the children attend school, and nuisances are abated. Such a society, acquainted with the town and all its people, would in great measure prevent the growth of pauperism, and it could give the wisest advice to private almsgivers were any almsgivers necessary, and it should make itself and its influence so prominent that all who wished to help others would come to it first for information and advice. Such an association formed when the town contained but a few inhabitants, would grow with its growth and would become the center and instigator of all good works, educational and elevating, that might be undertaken either by individuals or by the town itself. The main point in regard to the association is that each member should have but a small section of the town, the one directly in his own neighborhood, to study, and it is by means of this subdivision that the town may be assimilated to the country village.

In a city no such simple means will suffice—for

in every city the large multitudes of inhabitants and the complications of living make imposture easy, and unknown suffering a possibility, and a more complicated machinery is needed to defeat the one and discover the other.   I believe a "Charity Organization Society" to be a necessity in order to check the growth of pauperism in cities, and to guide charity toward wise measures.   In a country village, the mountain springs supply the water that is a necessity of life, and from the kind hearts of neighbors flows, also, a living stream of charity blessing those who receive it ; but in the city, unhappily, we need reservoirs and pipes, ramifying through all the streets, and branching up into every house to bring us even the water we drink, while in like manner even our love to our neighbor must be guided through organized channels, or it will lose its life-giving powers and become a source of moral disease and death.*

---

* The constitution and by-laws of the New York Charity Organization Society are recommended as a model.

CHAPTER IV.

PRACTICAL SUGGESTIONS.

The ways of putting the rules of true charitable work into practice are as many as are the human beings who need help, but there are certain classes of sufferers, the members of each of which may be dealt with by very much the same means and these it seems worth while to describe.

The classes of cases where direct money help may be given are confined to those where the natural breadwinner is dead, or disabled by physical ailment, and these may be divided into permanent, long continued, and temporary disability. In all these cases, before any such help is decided on, it must be clearly understood that it is better, in the long run, better morally, better for themselves and the community, that the family should be held together; otherwise, whatever the suffering, entering an institution public or private, is the remedy for their trouble.

Old people, who through no fault of their own, have come to poverty, and who have no children who ought to help them, may be made recipients of a weekly or monthly pension, but it should be sufficient for a comfortable living and should be given by individuals, if possible, upon whom they have some claim. Each case must be judged on its own merits. These I call cases requiring permanent relief.

Widows with young children require long continued relief, and this should be given, but with the greatest care; no regular pension paid out week by week, without individual supervision, will suffice—such can not fail to injure both the mother and children especially if it is supplied from public funds.

The position of a widow with small children whom she must support is most pitiful—she has to perform both the duties of father and mother, and in the nature of things she can not do it. If she devotes herself to earning a living for her children, they suffer for her care, and if she gives them the care they need, she and they have not food sufficient. Under these circumstances, it is not only an injury to her and to her children, but to the public, to leave her unaided, and to break up the family and scatter the children *may* be an unnecessary and unwise cruelty. Each case must be decided on its own merits, but if the mother is all she should be and can earn the support of the family, it is the office of true charity to pay some one else to do a mother's part to the children, and to care for the house. In the case of two widows

with children, they may be encouraged to help
each other by living together, the one doing the
inside work, the other earning the living of both
families so far as possible, supplemented by a certain sum from outside, which may be given as pay
for the services of the one woman in taking care
of the other's children. Constant oversight, however, is necessary in such arrangements, to see
that all goes well, that the children are cared for
and go to school, and to decide when, as the latter become able to help their mothers, the outside
help shall gradually be discontinued.

I know that many wise persons believe that
such a mode of dealing with widows encourages
improvidence in men; but we must not demand
too much of human nature, and it is not natural
that a young man should look forward to dying,
and he is scarcely more likely to insure his life,
or to lay by money, for fear that his children will
be sent to an institution after his death, than for
fear they will have to depend partly on outside
charity. We may encourage foresight and providence in other ways that bring less suffering to
the innocent and less injury to the community.

Temporary help may sometimes be given in
cases of sickness, especially if there are peculiarly
difficult and painful circumstances, but usually the
hospital is the best resort for the sick, for the cure
is more rapid and the habit of dependence is not

developed, which is far too often the case where direct money help is given, even with great care.

To help convalescents, with special diet, or by giving them change of air, are legitimate ways of administering charity, but in all and every case, it is necessary to know it thoroughly in order not to do harm, and it is infinitely better if the help given can come from an individual to an individual, from a friend to a friend, rather than from a Society to " a case."

The above classes of sufferers are all comparatively easy to deal with—help may be given if only care is exercised—and they are a great element of happiness to those who have charge of them, for they are allowed to relieve the suffering they see and their relations with those they help may be of a very close and tender character, rich in blessings to both.

We come now, however, to the most painful of all cases, those where the cause of suffering is moral, where the innocent suffer with the guilty, and where there seems almost nothing to be done. Often it is found that a whole family is suffering from the fault of the one man in all the world to whom they have a right to look for support and protection, and here the process of cure, if cure be possible, will be painful to all alike. The first thing to be understood, however, is that the wife and children of a drunkard *must* suffer, no power can prevent that; the only question presented is as to the kind of suffering. Shall the man be encouraged in his vileness, shall his children be exposed to the almost unimaginable horrors, moral and physical, which are inevitable so long as they live in the same house with him, shall there be children born yearly who will inherit broken health and depraved minds and bodies, and all this fostered by benevolence? Or shall the mother be forced, by her desire to see her children fed, to save them from this fate? Many good people call it a cruelty to refuse help to the family of a drunkard, but where the father and mother are cruel, no outside help will save the children from suffering, while to refuse outside help may do so.

I have not the slightest doubt that it is a *wrong*, and a great wrong, to give help to the family of a drunkard or an immoral man who will not support them. Unless the woman will remove her children from his influence, it should be understood that no public or private charity, and no charitable individual, has the right to help perpetuate and maintain such families as are brought forth by drunkards and vicious men and women.

The answer to objections on moral grounds that a woman has a duty to her husband which she must perform, is conclusive. She has no right to sacrifice her children to her husband—they are helpless and dependent upon her—he can reform if he chooses, or can at least voluntarily enter an institution where he will be helped to reform, and the strongest possible motive that he can have to reform is that his wife and children will suffer if he does not, or will leave him.

In case a woman does leave her husband from principle, she should be protected from him and should be treated as though she were a widow. In the case of drinking women, the rules should be the same, and every effort be made to save the husband and children from the discomforts and suffering consequent on her vice.

Deserted wives with children must not be treated as widows, for it has been found that to deal as tenderly with them as sympathy would dictate, leads other men to desert their families, trusting them to charitable care, and even induces husbands and wives to play upon the sympathies of the benevolent by pretended desertions. Therefore, in these sad cases, even when most pitiful, it is necessary for the general good, to be more severe than seems best sometimes for the individual.

Of course, where it is possible, the man should be dealt with by law and forced to support his family, but where he has escaped entirely, the mother and children should be left to be maintained by the constituted authorities, and the family broken up and distributed in different institutions, unless they can support themselves. It ought to be understood in every community that where a man deserts his wife and children and neglects his most pressing duties to them and to the public, that they will be left to suffer the fate he has prepared for them.

It can not be too often repeated that all these directions are general—that every case must be considered separately, and individually, and that every proposed plan must be scrutinized and its merits judged by the light of the first rule that the object of all charitable action must be *permanent benefit.*

Help by means of employment is one of the natural devices of those who wish to aid the poor without demoralizing them, but unfortunately, this method, like many other good things is open to abuse, and can not be carelessly resorted to. In order to judge of the wisdom of supplying artificial work as a permanent means of relieving the poor, the whole question of poverty must be looked at broadly. We have to go so far back as to ask, " What does the poverty of the worthy poor mean?" It can mean nothing else than that there are too many people in the community where the poverty exists. Sober, industrious men and women are poor only because their wages are low. If they can not get work it is because no one needs them, and if wages are low it is because there is such competition among the workers that they underbid each other. There is a congestion of workers wherever the "worthy poor" are suffering. For this state of things there seem but two remedies, one to create a genuine demand for their work on the spot where they are, and the other to send them to some place where a demand already exists. If a new industry can be created, a factory opened, or new land be brought into cultivation, the industrious and sober poor will cease to suffer for the time, or if they can all be colonized at some near or distant point where work at good wages is offered, the difficulty will be met. To undertake, however, to make artificial work for them, to supply charity sewing, or open a charity woodyard, is only to make matters worse than they were before, for the original poor people still remain where they were, and others, moreover, will probably come also to ask for employment, attracted by the offer of work, which is a great inducement to many who would scorn to ask or accept open charity.

A *labor-test* is a necessity, if able bodied men and women are to be helped, but it must be a labor-test only and the preliminary to finding them regular employment, and it must be disagreeable and under paid, or it will be no test.

Before leaving the question of work, it is well to call attention to the following facts : That, where there is an able-bodied man in the family, it is his duty to support himself, his wife and his children, and that only harm can result if efforts are made to induce the woman to leave her house daily for work. Her whole time is not too much to give to their care and that of the house, and what she earns can not compensate for the loss occasioned by her absence. Young children should also be kept from work. It injures them, and moreover, wherever women and children work as a rule. all wages, even the men's are reduced.

The second rule is that the best help of all is to help people to help themselves, and it follows that no amount of thought or time or money can be too much to spend on such help as this, and that all plans for starting provident schemes, for encouraging thrift, for teaching providence and self-control, for establishing schools for industrial training and the teaching of skill, especially such as will help not only that residuum which we technically call "the poor" but the whole community, are the best manifestations of true charity.

It is seldom remembered that the great scheme of Savings Banks was originally conceived and put into operation as a means of helping the poor.

The two first savings banks were started in Hamburg in 1778 and in Berne in 1787, and both were more or less closely restricted to the use of domestic servants, handicraftsmen and the like. The Hamburg bank was part of the general administration of the poor funds. In Tottenham, near London, the first British savings bank was started in 1798 by Priscilla Wakefield for children, and in 1804 it was extended to adults. In 1808 Lady Isabella Douglas founded a bank for servants in Bath. In 1810 Dr. Henry Duncan, a minister in Dumfriesshire, opened a bank, and in 1813 the first Edinburgh savings bank was started by the "Society for the Suppression of Beggars."

These examples are not often remembered or quoted. Savings banks have grown to be such immense business enterprises, and are so necessary a part of the life of every nation, that they are never thought of as a "charity"—but they should be constantly pointed to as an example of what true charity can do. Imagine the infinite difference between the results of that charity and any common soup-house or dole-giving charity. Sunday Schools are another example of the same sort of charity. Any and every scheme of real charity will have in it a germ of life that will cause it to live and grow and bless ever increasing thousands year by year, while the unhappy and demoralizing methods of trying to help the poor by encouraging them to rely on others will have to struggle on amidst an ever-growing crowd of miserable beings whom it creates and whom its efforts not only fail to bless, but whom it becomes yearly less able to cope with.

We have, then, our guiding principle :

That charity must tend to develop the moral

nature of those it helps, and must not tend to injure others ; and our two rules :

That each case must be dealt with radically, and a permanent means of helping it be found, and that the best way to help people is to help them to help themselves—and these seem simple enough, but to carry them out requires an amount of principle and character, of work and devotion, which it sometimes seems almost impossible to find. Besides the intimate knowledge of the suffering people which I have mentioned already as the necessary preliminary to all efficient help, the main instrument to be depended on to raise the standard of decency, cleanliness, providence and morality among them must be personal influence, which means that a constant and continued intercourse must be kept up between those who have a high standard and those who have it not, and that the educated and happy and good are to give some of their time regularly and as a duty, year in and year out, to the ignorant, the miserable and the vicious. In. a Christian community it ought not to be difficult to find those ready to undertake such a task, and unless they are found (men and women both), vice and crime will continue to grow by the side of poverty and wretchedness in the rich cities of our favored land.

POVERTY, U. S. A.

THE HISTORICAL RECORD

An Arno Press/New York Times Collection

Adams, Grace. **Workers on Relief.** 1939.

The Almshouse Experience: Collected Reports. 1821-1827.

Armstrong, Louise V. **We Too Are The People.** 1938.

Bloodworth, Jessie A. and Elizabeth J. Greenwood.
The Personal Side. 1939.

Brunner, Edmund de S. and Irving Lorge.
**Rural Trends in Depression Years: A Survey of
Village-Centered Agricultural Communities, 1930-1936.**
1937.

Calkins, Raymond.
**Substitutes for the Saloon: An Investigation Originally
made for The Committee of Fifty.** 1919.

Cavan, Ruth Shonle and Katherine Howland Ranck.
**The Family and the Depression: A Study of
One Hundred Chicago Families.** 1938.

Chapin, Robert Coit.
**The Standard of Living Among Workingmen's Families
in New York City.** 1909.

**The Charitable Impulse in Eighteenth Century America:
Collected Papers.** 1711-1797.

Children's Aid Society.
Children's Aid Society Annual Reports, 1-10.
February 1854-February 1863.

Conference on the Care of Dependent Children.
**Proceedings of the Conference on the Care
of Dependent Children.** 1909.

Conyngton, Mary.
How to Help: A Manual of Practical Charity. 1909.

Devine, Edward T. **Misery and its Causes.** 1909.

Devine, Edward T. **Principles of Relief.** 1904.

Dix, Dorothea L.
On Behalf of the Insane Poor: Selected Reports. 1843-1852.

Douglas, Paul H.
**Social Security in the United States: An Analysis and
Appraisal of the Federal Social Security Act.** 1936.

Farm Tenancy: Black and White. Two Reports. 1935, 1937.

Feder, Leah Hannah.
**Unemployment Relief in Periods of Depression:
A Study of Measures Adopted in Certain American
Cities, 1857 through 1922.** 1936.

Folks, Homer.
**The Care of Destitute, Neglected, and
Delinquent Children.** 1900.

Guardians of the Poor.
**A Compilation of the Poor Laws of the State of
Pennsylvania from the Year 1700 to 1788, Inclusive.** 1788.

Hart, Hastings, H.
Preventive Treatment of Neglected Children.
(Correction and Prevention, Vol. 4) 1910.

Herring, Harriet L.
**Welfare Work in Mill Villages: The Story of Extra-Mill
Activities in North Carolina.** 1929.

The Jacksonians on the Poor: Collected Pamphlets.
1822-1844.

Karpf, Maurice J.
Jewish Community Organization in the United States.
1938.

Kellor, Frances A.
Out of Work: A Study of Unemployment. 1915.

Kirkpatrick, Ellis Lore.
The Farmer's Standard of Living. 1929.

Komarovsky, Mirra.
The Unemployed Man and His Family: The Effect of Unemployment Upon the Status of the Man in Fifty-Nine Families. 1940.

Leupp, Francis E. **The Indian and His Problem.** 1910.

Lowell, Josephine Shaw.
Public Relief and Private Charity. 1884.

More, Louise Bolard.
Wage Earners' Budgets: A Study of Standards and Cost of Living in New York City. 1907.

New York Association for Improving the Condition of the Poor.
AICP First Annual Reports Investigating Poverty. 1845-1853.

O'Grady, John.
Catholic Charities in the United States: History and Problems. 1930.

Raper, Arthur F.
Preface to Peasantry: A Tale of Two Black Belt Counties. 1936.

Raper, Arthur F. **Tenants of The Almighty.** 1943.

Richmond, Mary E.
What is Social Case Work? An Introductory Description. 1922.

Riis, Jacob A. **The Children of the Poor.** 1892.

Rural Poor in the Great Depression: Three Studies. 1938.

Sedgwick, Theodore.
Public and Private Economy: Part I. 1836.

Smith, Reginald Heber. **Justice and the Poor.** 1919.

Sutherland, Edwin H. and Harvey J. Locke.
Twenty Thousand Homeless Men: A Study of Unemployed Men in the Chicago Shelters. 1936.

Tuckerman, Joseph.
On the Elevation of the Poor: A Selection From His Reports as Minister at Large in Boston. 1874.

Warner, Amos G. **American Charities.** 1894.

Watson, Frank Dekker.
The Charity Organization Movement in the United States: A Study in American Philanthropy. 1922.

Woods, Robert A., et al. **The Poor in Great Cities.** 1895.